Medicaid
and Other Experiments
in State Health Policy

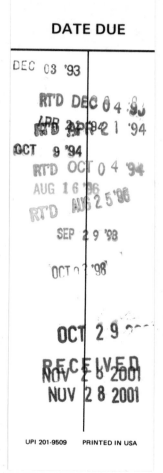

Medicaid
and Other Experiments
in State Health Policy

Rosemary Gibson Kern
and
Susan R. Windham

with
Paula Griswold

American Enterprise Institute for Public Policy Research
Washington, D.C.

Rosemary Gibson Kern is a research associate in AEI's Center for Health Policy Research. Susan Windham is a Boston-based consultant. Paula Griswold is health policy director for the Massachusetts Business Roundtable.

This volume was prepared under a grant from the Pew Memorial Trust, for whose support the authors are grateful.

Library of Congress Cataloging-in-Publication Data

Kern, Rosemary Gibson.
  Medicaid and other experiments in state health policy.

  (AEI studies ; 437)
    1. Medical care—Massachusetts—Cost control.
2. Medicaid—Massachusetts—Cost control.   3. Medicaid—
Finance—Congresses.   4. Medicare—Finance—Congresses.
I. Windham, Susan.   II. Griswold, Paula.   III. American
Enterprise Institute for Public Policy Research.
IV. Title.   V. Series.   [DNLM: 1. Cost control.   2. De-
livery of Health Care—economics—Massachusetts.
3. Economics, Hospital—Massachusetts.   4. Health Policy—
Massachusetts.   5. Medical Assistance, Title 19—

1 3 5 7 9 10 8 6 4 2

ISBN 0-8447-3595-7

AEI Studies 437

 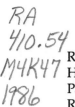
Printed in the United St~¹

Contents

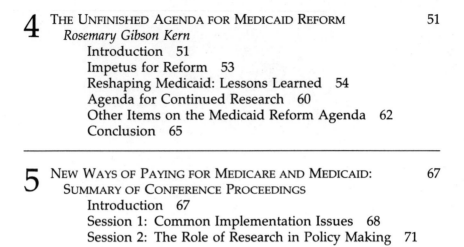

Foreword

This volume continues the work that began three years ago when AEI's Center for Health Policy Research conducted a survey of state initiatives in Medicaid reform and published its findings in *Restructuring Medicaid: A Survey of State and Local Initiatives.* In this volume the authors examine other initiatives in greater depth and discuss additional items on the Medicaid reform agenda.

The first three chapters are case studies of three Massachusetts initiatives—regulatory and market based—to control the rate of increase in health care expenditures. The first case study traces the development and implementation of a Medicaid case management program that grew out of a federal demonstration. The second case study highlights the impetus for, and subsequent dissolution of, the Commonwealth Health Care Corporation, a Medicaid experiment proposed by Boston health care providers to expand patients' access to care and to control expenditures. The third case study examines the development and status of the state's first global hospital budgeting system that regulates hospital revenues and charges.

Chapter 4 highlights some criteria for evaluating Medicaid initiatives. Evaluators need to determine whether health care resources can be used more cost effectively and, at the same time, whether patients can be assured of the same, if not better, access to care. It also raises additional items on the Medicaid reform agenda such as ways to redress inequities among states' Medicaid programs.

Chapter 5 summarizes the proceedings of a conference in which researchers discussed preliminary findings from their analyses of demonstration projects that test new ways of paying for care under public programs.

This focus on state health policy making is part of AEI's work in the Center for Health Policy Research to examine questions that are at the forefront of the policy debate. In *Incentives versus Controls in Health Policy,* edited by Jack A. Meyer, lessons learned from other sectors of the economy are applied to current health policy issues such as price determination, cost control, and access to health care services. Another volume, *Current Trends in Health Care,* edited by

Marion Ein Lewin, contains essays on such issues as meeting the long-term care needs of the growing elderly population and devising an ethical framework for allocating resources to provide care to those who are without health insurance. In *Managing Health Care Costs*, Sean Sullivan presents case studies on companies and coalitions that have been trend setters in cost containment efforts in the private sector. This volume examines the trend setters in the public sector.

WILLIAM J. BAROODY
President
American Enterprise Institute

Introduction

States have undertaken a variety of experiments to control the rate of increase in health care expenditures. In the early 1980s Medicaid expenditures in many states began to account for a growing portion of their budgets. In fact, in many states, Medicaid was the fastest growing item in the budget. Some states tried to control the rate of increase in expenditures by cutting benefits, limiting eligibility, and squeezing provider reimbursement.

Other states have tried alternative approaches to controlling health care expenditures by organizing more efficient delivery and financing of services. This volume examines several of these alternative strategies. It also examines a more wide-reaching effort to control health expenditures by setting limits on hospitals' revenues through state rate regulation.

Susan Windham and Paula Griswold trace a combination of regulatory and case management initiatives developed in Massachusetts, where health expenditures are 30 percent above the national average. One initiative, the Massachusetts Medicaid case management program, has been operating since the mid-1970s and grew out of a federal demonstration. It attempts to organize the delivery of health care services by encouraging providers and patients to use resources judiciously.

Another Massachusetts experiment, the Commonwealth Health Care Corporation (CHCC), was spearheaded by a consortium of providers whose purpose was to develop an alternative way of delivering and financing care to Medicaid beneficiaries in the face of a threat by the state to make massive cuts in the state's Medicaid budget. The providers rejected traditional means of cost control, such as limiting payment rates and reducing benefits. They proposed, instead, to enroll Medicaid recipients in a managed health care program to enable providers to deliver care more efficiently. The case study summarizes the events that marked CHCC's short history and documents the reasons for its demise. An analysis of the reasons can help policy makers understand the political and technical issues that arise in developing alternative delivery and financing systems.

1

A third Massachusetts effort to control expenditures—a global hospital budgeting system—was enacted in August 1982 with strong support from the business community. It sought to replace the cost reimbursement system with a system whereby each hospital's budget is set in advance. The incentive effects are analyzed and compared with Medicare's diagnosis related group (DRG) payment system. An update on the current status of the program is presented since Medicare is no longer included in the hospital payment system.

Rosemary Gibson Kern discusses some of the lessons learned from several states' efforts to manage the care received by Medicaid patients. The test of the experiments is whether they can assure quality of care, pay providers sufficiently to encourage their participation, and control the rate of increase in expenditures. Other needed Medicaid reforms are also discussed. Numerous inequities exist among the states' programs, some of which can be redressed by federal and state efforts. Several options are highlighted.

The last chapter summarizes the proceedings of a conference on Medicaid and Medicare reform made possible by a grant from the Pew Memorial Trust. At the conference state officials discussed the steps being taken to change the structure of Medicaid financing and delivery, and researchers evaluating Medicare and Medicaid demonstrations discussed ways of disseminating their research findings to states trying to implement new programs.

1

The Massachusetts Medicaid
Case Management Program

Susan R. Windham

The Massachusetts Medicaid Case Management Program (CMP) began in 1977 as a demonstration funded by the Health Care Financing Administration (HCFA) for four years. The primary goal of the demonstration was to test a model of health care delivery that attempted to reduce or contain costs for Medicaid recipients while maintaining a high quality of care. The program was similar to a health maintenance organization (HMO) in that participants enrolled voluntarily with a provider who was to deliver or coordinate all the health care services they received.

This case study summarizes the major provision of the CMP and reports on its current status. Because of the program's success during the four-year demonstration period, the Massachusetts Department of Public Welfare (DPW) decided to continue case management as one option for delivering health care services to its Medicaid population. The program is worthy of study as a market-based—as opposed to a regulatory—approach to containing health care costs. Moreover, it offers insights into the effectiveness of HMO models of care as ways of serving low-income populations cost effectively.

The author gratefully acknowledges the contributions of the following persons in the preparation of this report: Jan Singer, former director, Managed Health Development Unit, Medicaid Division, Massachusetts Department of Public Welfare; Sarah Bachman, former director, Managed Health Development Demonstration Project, Medicaid Division, Massachusetts Department of Public Welfare; and Hunter McKay, director of research and program development, Managed Health Development Unit, Medicaid Division, Massachusetts Department of Public Welfare.

Description of the Program

The Case Management Program began when the HCFA authorized the Department of Public Welfare to develop and test managed medical care delivery among recipients of Aid to Families with Dependent Children (AFDC) in the state's Medicaid program. The program had several objectives:

- to determine whether case management reduced the costs of medical care for Medicaid recipients and their use of care
- to assess consumers' satisfaction with this kind of program
- to provide high quality care
- to assess the effectiveness of the incentives used by the program in changing providers' and consumers' behavior

The success of the program depended on three groups: the DPW, which pays for Medicaid services and initiated and monitored the program; the provider organizations, which were responsible for developing on-site systems and procedures for offering case-managed care; and the Medicaid recipients, who voluntarily enrolled at primary care sites, agreeing to restrict their medical care to those sites.

The DPW used economic incentives to motivate both providers and enrollees to participate in the program. Providers were promised a share of any savings from the provision of case-managed care. Each enrollee was given seven dollars every month he or she remained in the program. DPW representatives believe, however, that noneconomic incentives played a major role in encouraging participation. For providers, these may have included the opportunity to participate in an innovative program, a way to increase the number of patients served, and the availability of consultant and technical services from DPW program staff on issues related to managed care. For enrollees, noneconomic incentives included the chance to have their own physicians and maintain an ongoing relationship with them.

Each provider signed a case management contract with the state, which incorporated guidelines for implementation and compliance. Enrollees were given handbooks that explained the program's requirements and restraints. The greatest challenge for providers was to develop and institute a method for tracking patients to limit unnecessary care. Only by tracking patients could the provider site disallow claims for care received without prior approval of the primary care physician (case manager). Each tracking system required careful documentation of all medical care received both at the primary care site and through referrals. Because it was easier to monitor enrollees at the primary care site than to follow them through a referral, a closely coordinated referral system was also critical. The tracking systems required procedures for

- ensuring that a central record of referrals was kept
- ensuring that enrollees were aware of any referrals made on their behalf
- notifying consulting physicians of referrals and obtaining feedback from them
- receiving a record of the outcome of referrals

Case manager physicians were the core of the program: they were responsible for the prudent buying of health care on behalf of the enrollee and the DPW and for coordinating all other aspects of service delivery. Their responsibilities were to

- provide health maintenance care
- request return visits
- order/coordinate ancillaries
- make referrals to specialists
- determine need/refer for hospitalization
- determine need/coordinate home care, long-term care, and rehabilitation services

Along with the DPW's ability to deny payment for inappropriate care, the primary care physicians were the major controls on the delivery of cost-effective care.

During the first two years of the demonstration, six case management sites were established: one hospital-affiliated health center, one hospital outpatient department, three neighborhood health centers, and one private group practice.

The Hahnemann Family Health Center (HFHC) was the first site to sign a case management contract. The only family practice residency program in the state, it is affiliated with Worcester Hahnemann Hospital. Enrollment began at HFHC in August 1979, and operation of the program ceased at this site in October 1980.

The Beth Israel Ambulatory Care Center (BIAC) and the Children's Hospital Comprehensive Child Care Program (CHCCP) jointly formed the second case management site. Both are ambulatory care centers in Boston teaching hospitals. Case management enrollees were to be served cooperatively, adult care being provided by BIAC and pediatric care by CHCCP. The first enrollees joined the program at BIAC/CHCCP in September 1979, and the demonstration ended at this site in October 1981.

The South End Community Health Center (SECHC) and Uphams Corner Health Center (UCHC) were the third and fourth sites to join case management. Both are free-standing neighborhood health centers that serve many Medicaid recipients in Boston. Operation of the program began in November 1979 at SECHC and in December 1979 at UCHC; the demonstration ended at these sites in October 1981.

Case management contracts for the fifth site were signed with two group practices in Springfield, a city in western Massachusetts. This was a joint site, where adult care was provided by the Hampden County Medical Group (HCMG) and pediatric care by Valley Pediatrics (VP). To encourage this site's participation, both HCMG and VP were permitted to bill Medicaid at a higher rate during the program's operation. They participated on a risk-sharing basis; that is, they were at risk for a proportion of the dollars spent, over a set limit, for enrollees. Operation of the program at HCMG/VP began in December 1980 and continued until October 1981.

The final case management site was the Roxbury Comprehensive Community Health Center (RCCHC), a neighborhood health center that serves a large Medicaid population in Boston. It also was at risk for a proportion of the dollars spent, over a set limit, for case management enrollees. Enrollment began at RCCHC in December 1980 and continued until the demonstration ended in October 1981.

These sites were chosen for specific reasons. First, each site already provided comprehensive care. If enrollees were to be restricted to a single case management site for their total health care, complete primary care had to be available at that site. Second, each case management site already served Medicaid recipients; moreover, each either had a large number of AFDC patients when it joined the program or was willing to increase the number during case management. Third, these sites appeared to have the potential to save money under case management. During contract negotiations, a profile of the utilization history of patients eligible for the program was completed. Most of these profiles revealed that the patients had received less than 50 percent of their primary care at the case management site. Therefore, the sites seemed to have a good chance of saving money if they became the major source of care and the use of other health providers could be curtailed. Finally, during contract negotiations, each site indicated its willingness to comply with the programs' policies by developing and using systems that would enable it to provide cost-effective, continuous, and high-quality health care to enrollees.

Policies Related to Cost-Effectiveness. The DPW was to develop the necessary administrative structure to support the delivery of cost-effective care in the case management sites. A major aspect of this structure was the ability to pay only those claims for care that was provided or authorized by the case manager; however, a system for disallowing claims was developed only at the last two sites. The system was not established at the other four sites for several reasons.

During the planning stages, the DPW did not have a computer system sophisticated enough to review claims as required by the demonstration project, although a Medicaid management information system (MMIS) that would be capable of doing so was being developed for the department.[1] The grant staff assumed that the MMIS would be functional by the time the program began and continued to plan for a system claims review.

At the same time, many providers who were interested in participating in case management objected strongly to denying payment to other health care facilities that served their patients without receiving prior approval. They were reluctant to put themselves in the uncomfortable position of denying revenue to their colleagues or having revenue denied to their own facilities. The DPW also hesitated actually to deny payment for claims, but it did want a system in place to defer off-site claims for case management enrollees until it was determined that the care had been properly authorized. Staff members hoped that the delay required to scrutinize claims before payment would discourage off-site providers from delivering nonemergency, nonreferral services to program enrollees.

Later in the program operation, two events facilitated the development of a system for deferring claims. First, as the demonstration was coming to an end, the state considered developing its own ongoing version of case management. Recognizing the need for both programs to have a claims deferral system, the DPW began to work closely with the grant staff to develop such a system. Second, the DPW wanted the last two case management sites to join on a risk-sharing basis. These sites were willing to share the risk only if the DPW established a system that would enable them to disallow claims for inappropriate care. They were more afraid of losing money than of offending their peers by denying claims.

The DPW's claims processing center examined all claims for care provided to enrollees from these two sites and separated claims that did not originate at the enrollee's site from those coming from the case manager. Claims from the site were automatically paid; those from other providers were deferred and forwarded to the primary care site. The staff determined, on the basis of information in a twenty-four-hour call-in log sheet and medical records, whether the claims should be paid or disallowed. Claims from other providers were paid if they were for emergency treatment or approved referrals. The claims to be disallowed were reviewed by staff at each primary care site so

7

they could reiterate to enrollees that they must receive care that is authorized by their case manager. The claims were then returned to the department's claims processing center, where they were paid or not according to each site's determination. Off-site providers were informed if payment was denied.

This procedure was somewhat cumbersome because the major tasks were performed manually, increasing the probability of error. The system could not handle a procedure for prior approval of claims, even though this would greatly have improved its efficiency. Nonetheless, this rudimentary system did allow the DPW and case management providers to deny payment to other providers for nonreferral off-site care—a basic case management requirement.

The lack of a systematic claims review system at the first four sites made it nearly impossible to determine when their enrollees received out-of-plan care. For a short while, the program staff attempted to track enrollees without the use of a computer. Claims were matched to the referral log, and some out-of-plan use was pinpointed. It usually required three to four months, however, to gather all the claims and determine which were for out-of-plan care. Within a year the manual process was dropped at these sites because it was cumbersome and did not provide timely information that could be used to disallow claims. As a result, there is little evidence that physicians at the first four sites changed the way in which they delivered care during the demonstration.

Results

During the entire demonstration period at all the sites, 2,842 AFDC cases enrolled in the Case Management Program—92.4 percent of the total adjusted goal of 3,075 cases.[2] The sites had varied success in meeting enrollment goals; the last two to join were the most successful, exceeding their adjusted goals.

In the evaluation by the state, the data on costs and use showed that case management was successful to some degree at every site. In accordance with expectations, significant changes in the use of health care occurred. Average total costs for enrollees were reduced at all sites while costs for control groups showed no significant change at three sites, an increase at one site, and slight decreases that did not compare to the large decreases for enrollees at two sites. The use of ambulatory care increased at every site while among controls at four of the six sites no change in use occurred.

Off-site ambulatory care costs for enrollees decreased significantly at all six sites; for controls they increased at two sites, did not change significantly at two, and declined very slightly at two. Off-site ambulatory and outpatient department use by enrollees dropped at every site; use by control groups increased or did not change.

Hospital costs and utilization rates dropped in some way at every site for both enrollees and controls. Hospital costs fell significantly at six sites for enrollees and at five for controls. The average number of hospital admissions was reduced significantly for both enrollees and controls at five sites. Only at Hahnemann were there significant reductions in length of hospital stay and average number of admissions for enrollees with no significant change for the control group. It is difficult to conclude that case management alone was responsible for the change in hospital costs and use for enrollees since controls demonstrated very similar changes.

Current Status and Future Plans

A unit was created in the DPW in 1981 to continue the managed-care program—now called the Health Connection—as an ongoing responsibility and to try to expand it. Formal means were developed for marketing the program to increase enrollment and for correcting systems problems that had been identified during the demonstration period. The department's position was that if success had been achieved with rudimentary systems for monitoring out-of-plan use, restricting payment, and so on, the impact of the program would be dramatic once critical system components were in place. The current program emphasizes reducing use as well as costs. With the inception of Chapter 372, the Massachusetts global hospital budgeting system, reimbursement of providers in the state was heavily regulated; therefore, use has become a better measure of the effect of case management than cost savings.

The Case Management Program now has about 10,000 enrollees, all voluntarily enrolled. According to staff members, enrollees join to maintain a close relationship with a provider and like the idea of having their "own" physicians. To increase enrollment further, the DPW has asked the secretary of the U.S. Department of Health and Human Services for permission to increase the seven-dollar-per-month incentive fee to twenty-five dollars per family per month every six months if they stay in the program for at least six months.[3] The staff maintains that this increase reflects its desire to "share the cost savings" of the program with enrollees, much as HMOs share their cost savings with providers and enrollees (through lower premiums than traditional health insurance).

Of the six original sites, three have continued to serve as pro-

9

viders of case-managed care: the South End Community Health Center, the Roxbury Comprehensive Community Health Center, and the Uphams Corner Health Center. Other health centers have joined the program. A dental program and a disabled program, which is being operated as an experiment with a Boston medical group, have been added. The disabled program provides case-managed care to persons with spinal cord injuries; there is a control group in the western part of the state. With grant support from the Robert Wood Johnson Foundation, the Boston University School of Public Health is evaluating the effectiveness of this component.

In the years since the fully developed program began operation, the DPW reports that all sites have saved the state money, costing less than expected expenditures per Medicaid beneficiary. Sites are paid bonuses of three dollars a month for each family enrolled. Bonuses are also paid to efficient sites. On the basis of the percentage of projected costs saved, sites are labeled high savers, low savers, and no savers. High savers have saved 15 percent or more of the projected average cost per case, low savers between 5 percent and 15 percent, and no savers less than 5 percent.

High savers receive seven dollars per case per month as a bonus after all savings calculations are completed. This is in addition to the three-dollar monthly incentive payment to all case management providers. Low savers receive four dollars per case per month as a savings bonus in addition to the incentive payment.

No savers stop receiving the three-dollar incentive payment as soon as the completed savings calculation shows no savings. A site will owe the DPW the total incentive payment for every year in which there are no savings. It will not receive further incentive payments until the previous year's payments are returned. If the site shows savings in subsequent years, bonus payments will be paid accordingly, and monthly incentive payments will resume as soon as all debts are settled for the years of no savings. If a provider drops out of the Case Management Program still owing money, the debt is subtracted from the DPW's fee-for-service payments to the provider over a period of twelve months (see figure 1).

In the near future, the DPW plans to add several new components to the Health Connection: a physician sponsor component, ambulatory capitation, managed care for the elderly in the community, and managed care for the frail elderly. The major features of these proposed additions are summarized in table 1.

The Physician Sponsor Model. To include independent physicians and their Medicaid clients in the managed health program, it has

FIGURE 1

SAVINGS INCENTIVES

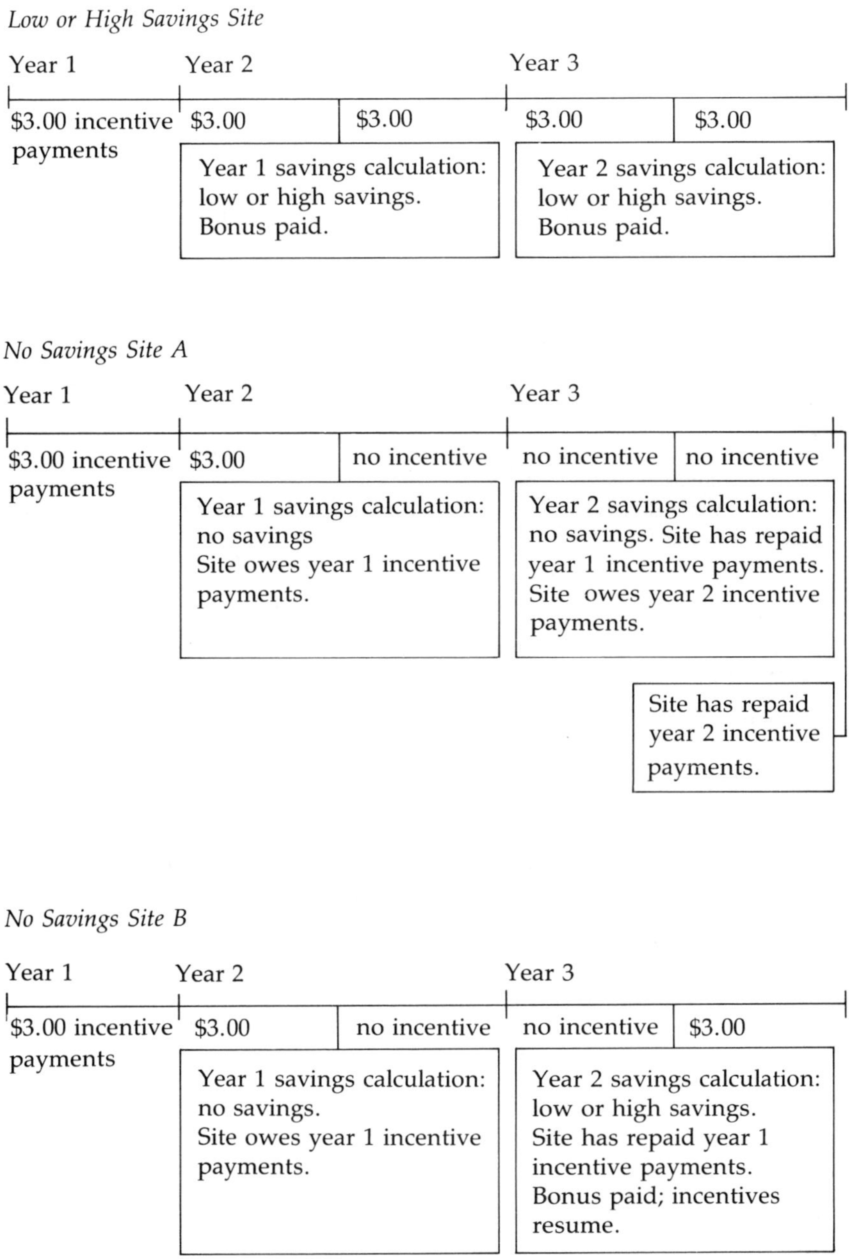

Low or High Savings Site

Year 1	Year 2		Year 3	
$3.00 incentive payments	$3.00	$3.00	$3.00	$3.00
	Year 1 savings calculation: low or high savings. Bonus paid.		Year 2 savings calculation: low or high savings. Bonus paid.	

No Savings Site A

Year 1	Year 2		Year 3	
$3.00 incentive payments	$3.00	no incentive	no incentive	no incentive
	Year 1 savings calculation: no savings Site owes year 1 incentive payments.		Year 2 savings calculation: no savings. Site has repaid year 1 incentive payments. Site owes year 2 incentive payments.	
				Site has repaid year 2 incentive payments.

No Savings Site B

Year 1	Year 2		Year 3	
$3.00 incentive payments	$3.00	no incentive	no incentive	$3.00
	Year 1 savings calculation: no savings. Site owes year 1 incentive payments.		Year 2 savings calculation: low or high savings. Site has repaid year 1 incentive payments. Bonus paid; incentives resume.	

TABLE 1

NEW HEALTH CONNECTION INITIATIVES

Physician Sponsor Model

Goals
- Initiate independent physician participation in managed health
- Allow recipients who have private physicians to participate in managed health
- Decrease use of institutional providers for specialist ambulatory care

Eligible Providers
- Private individual physicians
- Group practices

Client Population
- All AFDC recipients

Benefits
- Case-managed primary care
- All other benefits covered under Medicaid except dental, vision, long-term care and drugs

Reimbursement
- Fee for service at Medicaid rate
- A $3 per enrollee per month management fee
- Potential portions of savings

Evaluation
- Comparison of cost, use, and quality of care between recipients enrolled with a physician and nonenrolled recipients

Ambulatory Capitation

Goals
- Furnish incentives for physicians to provide case-managed care
- Reduce unnecessary inpatient days/or services
- Promote use of the most cost-efficient providers

Eligible Providers
- Private physicians
- Group practice associations
- Neighborhood health centers

Client Population
- Initial enrollment for AFDC recipients only—AFDC-Medicaid, Medical Assistance-AFDC, and Medical Assistance-Under 21

Benefits
- Enrollees to continue to receive covered Medicaid benefits; the case manager to supply or refer to almost all services
- Dental, vision, long-term care, and drugs excluded

Reimbursement
- Monthly tabulating of capitation payments to cover all or most non-inpatient services
- Annual shared savings check to case managers for decreased inpatient use
- Inpatient services reimbursed by Medicaid on a fee-for-service basis

Evaluation
- Cost, use, and quality of care
- Client selection
- Effect of catastrophic illness

Case Management for the Community Elderly

Goals
- Increase the quality of care through better management of health services delivery while containing costs

Eligible Providers
- Community health centers
- Primary care physician group practices
- Hospital-based ambulatory care centers

Client Population
- Medicaid recipients aged sixty-five and older who reside in the community

Benefits
- All Medicaid reimbursable health care services except for dental care and institutional long-term care

Reimbursement
- Fee-for-service reimbursement for all services delivered at the provider's site
- $3.00 management fee per enrollee per month
- No risk and no savings calculation

Evaluation
- After twelve to eighteen months of operation, evaluation of changes in cost, use, and quality of health care services

Frail Elderly

Goals
- Prevent inappropriate institutionalization

- Integrate health and social service delivery systems
- Increase effectiveness and efficiency of resource allocation

Eligible Providers
- Home care agencies
- Home health agencies
- Neighborhood health centers

Client Population
- Elderly Medicaid recipients who qualify for nursing home placement

Benefits
- Mix of community services that meets both health and social needs

Reimbursement
- Risk-free capitation based on a percentage of the cost of nursing home care

Evaluation
- Cost, use, and quality of care
- Community coordination and capacity building
- Client selection

---

become necessary to amend the requirements of the program. Managed health has contracted mainly with institutional providers, such as community health centers and hospital primary care departments. These contracts have imposed substantial administrative responsibilities on the providers who chose to participate. Even contracts with medical group practices have retained a heavy administrative burden. Solo practicing physicians and small group practices cannot easily manage this burden; therefore, managed health models that depend on changes in billing practices, complex utilization reporting, or financial risk are inappropriate for the independent physician. A similar model that retains managed health incentives to improve care and contain costs is more appropriate.

The sponsor model is designed to

- initiate participation of independent physicians in managed health
- encourage recipients who use private physicians to enroll in managed health
- facilitate enrollment of individuals instead of entire families
- decrease the use of institutional providers for specialist ambulatory care

In the physician sponsor model, an individual recipient voluntarily enrolls with an individual physician or a small group practice. The enrollee receives a restricted Medicaid card that limits him or her

14

to health care services provided or arranged for by the managing physician. The managing physician is responsible for coordinating all medical care delivered to the enrollee: providing services directly and making referrals for specialty care and hospitalization when necessary. In return for managing the care of enrollees, the physician receives a management fee of three dollars per family or one dollar per enrollee per month. If the program is successful in controlling costs and use, physicians may receive a bonus payment reflecting the costs saved.

The physician sponsor model differs from the original managed health model in the monitoring and evaluation component. Physician case managers will be required to keep a much more limited referral list, which includes referrals to institutional providers only. Referrals to noninstitutional providers need not be recorded. The DPW will compare the referral list with institutional claims monthly and deny payment for claims not approved by the managing physician. This reduction in paperwork should allow solo physicians to participate in managed health. It should also encourage them to refer patients to noninstitutional providers, which are less expensive.

Quality and access requirements will also be less burdensome. Solo physicians will not be required to keep a phone log, but they will be required to offer twenty-four hour coverage and to list any emergency calls that lead to the use of institutional health care services.

Ambulatory Capitation. Under the ambulatory capitation model, a Medicaid recipient enrolls with a physician, physician group, community health center, or HMO. The enrollee is issued a restricted Medicaid card and agrees to have all his or her care provided or arranged for by the case manager. In return for providing or coordinating and monitoring all medical care, the case manager receives a monthly capitation payment to cover all ambulatory costs. All inpatient costs for referrals are billed directly by the hospitals to the DPW on a fee-for-service basis.

A small percentage of the ambulatory capitation payment is withheld each month. At the end of the contract year, actual ambulatory and inpatient costs are calculated. If they are no higher than those projected, all withheld funds are returned to the case manager. If inpatient days have declined, a special bonus is paid to the case manager; if ambulatory costs have risen while inpatient days have declined, the increase in ambulatory costs is subtracted from the inpatient savings bonus.

Community Elderly. Case management for the community elderly proposes to extend case management to a new group of Medicaid recipients. The major objective is to provide appropriate, comprehensive, cost-effective primary care to elderly Medicaid recipients who reside in the community. The DPW hopes to achieve the same success in the elderly program as in the AFDC program: shifts in the pattern of health care use resulting in reduced costs.

Case management for the community elderly is one part of a continuum of care developed to meet the long-term care needs of all Medicaid recipients sixty-five and over. Services that must be available to enrollees either by referral or through on-site care by the case manager include gynecology, laboratory services, medicine, inpatient and outpatient hospital care, emergency services, speech, hearing, and vision care, and medically necessary transportation. Case management providers must be able to provide or arrange for services particularly important to some elderly persons—home health care, private duty nursing, physical and occupational therapy, and adult day health care. The only services that need not be covered are dental care and institutional long-term care.

Frail Elderly. The objective of this program is to offer to elderly Medicaid recipients a community-based alternative to nursing home care that costs Medicaid less than institutional placement. The delivery system has case management as a core service. Services will be authorized by an interdisciplinary case management staff functioning as (1) assessors of need, (2) gatekeepers to service, (3) quality assurance coordinators, and (4) payers for care.

For this program, all Medicaid-issued eligibility and entrance criteria, admissions procedures, and restrictions on use will be disregarded. Access to the services included will be determined by the interdisciplinary case management team, except for nursing home placement. Alternative care will include adult day care service, adult foster care, home health care, and private duty nursing.

Notes

1. Because of various departmental problems, plans for the development of the MMIS were postponed indefinitely in April 1980. Although the case management staff wanted a claims deferral system established immediately, it was not a priority for other departments in the DPW. The demonstration program was a small part of the department's many responsibilities.

2. Data in this section were taken from Sarah Bachman et al., "Case Management as a Cost-effective Approach to Improved Health Services Delivery

to Medicaid Recipients" (evaluation report of the Case Management Program), November 1982.

3. This approval must be received to avoid interference with the income eligibility required for receipt of welfare benefits.

2

The Commonwealth
Health Care Corporation:
A Medicaid Cost-Containment
Experiment in Boston

Susan R. Windham and Paula Griswold

Preface

The purpose of this case study is to analyze the issues that led to the dissolution of the Commonwealth Health Care Corporation (CHCC), a Medicaid cost-containment experiment proposed by health care providers in Boston. We have avoided taking a position on whether the program should have continued since we want the study to be educational rather than editorial.

In preparing the study, we reviewed program documents from Massachusetts state agencies, documents from CHCC, and numerous

We would like to thank the following persons and organizations for providing information for the case study: Dennis Beatrice, formerly with the Massachusetts Medicaid program, now with the Health Policy Consortium, Heller School, Brandeis University; Manuel Carballo, former secretary, Massachusetts Executive Office of Human Services; Mark Coven, formerly an attorney with Boston Legal Services and chairman, State Medicaid Advisory Panel; currently director of program and policy, Massachusetts Executive Office of Human Services; Myrtle Davis, former director, Harvard Street Neighborhood Health Center; Jon Kingsdale, Blue Cross of Massachusetts Inc., Division of Health Planning; Michael Koetting, former director of finance, CHCC; now with Abt Associates, Cambridge, Massachusetts; Massachusetts League of Neighborhood Health Centers, Boston; Diane Mazonson, Senate staff assistant, Massachusetts State House; Dr. Mitchell Rabkin, former president of the board, CHCC; chief executive officer, Beth Israel Hospital of Boston; The Robert Wood Johnson Foundation, Princeton, New Jersey; Barry Scheur, former director, Boston Health Plan, Boston City Hospital; Janet Singer, di-

articles written about CHCC and conducted interviews with persons involved with the program. A number of those interviewed preferred not to be named or quoted directly; we have therefore written the study without naming any of the key participants in the program. Although we have used some titles to assign specific responsibility for certain decisions or actions, we describe a "scenario" rather than individual participants. We feel that an understanding of the CHCC scenario has more educational value for other Medicaid reform efforts.

Overview

The spring of 1981 was an unsettling time for Massachusetts health care providers. President Ronald Reagan had singled out Medicaid, the federal health insurance program for the nation's low-income and disabled persons, for large budget reductions. In Massachusetts the conservative Democratic administration of Governor Edward King had chosen to follow the president's lead; a ceiling, or cap, had been proposed for the state's Medicaid budget, which had increased nearly 50 percent in three years, to more than $900 million. The cap would have cut Medicaid spending in Massachusetts by nearly $250 million, on the basis of assertions that one quarter of the state's Medicaid budget was spent unnecessarily. Some of the proposed savings would have been realized by tightening state Medicaid eligibility standards— in effect reducing the number of recipients, largely the working poor— and others through reductions in service coverage and through expected administrative efficiencies. Massachusetts cities and towns outside Boston generally favored the proposed cap; their Medicaid populations were smaller, and the governor had promised to share the expected savings among them. Providers of medical care, however, especially in Boston, had a sense of impending crisis.

The threat galvanized a group of Boston teaching hospitals into creating the Commonwealth Health Care Corporation (CHCC), a consortium of providers whose purpose was to develop and implement an innovative, cost-effective way to deliver health care services to the Boston Medicaid population. The program is worthy of study for several reasons. First, it was a cooperative effort of the private and the public sectors. Second, its purpose was to initiate a major structural reform in the health care delivery system. Finally, it is of interest

---

rector of case management programs, Massachusetts Department of Public Welfare; Rina Spence, former executive director, CHCC; independent consultant; and Stephen Weiner, former chief counsel, CHCC; attorney, Goulston and Storrs, Boston.

as a study in implementation; after an investment of two years and nearly $1 million, the program was terminated without having enrolled or provided services to a single Medicaid recipient.

This case study summarizes the significant events of CHCC's short history and attempts to document the major reasons for its demise. An analysis of these reasons may help policy makers or providers contemplating similar initiatives to understand the political and technical issues that arise in developing such programs and to identify the elements that are critical to successful implementation.

The first section describes the circumstances leading to the formation of CHCC and the period during which support and resources were assembled for program planning. The second section offers some detail on the components of the program, the planned operation, and the project staff. The third section outlines the work plan for development and identifies the constituencies that were or should have been recognized in the development phase. The fourth section describes and analyzes the events leading to the termination of the program. The final section draws some conclusions about the lessons to be learned from this attempt.

Background

The idea of CHCC originated in January 1981, when the administration of Governor King began discussions about setting a fixed budget for the Medicaid program. In conjunction with the proposed cap, state officials were soliciting from private sector groups statements of interest in setting up health care programs that would assume some of the financial risks of treating Medicaid patients. The election of Governor King reflected public support for the notion that there was significant fat in the state's welfare budget and that the private sector could provide services and control costs more effectively than the public sector.

Gaining some control over the allocation of the state Medicaid budget certainly appealed to the hospitals, particularly in an era of increasing competition among medical providers and pressure from public payers and private insurers to control costs. The hospitals were searching for ways to guarantee a steady, predictable flow of revenue to their institutions, while exploring fresh ideas for improving efficiency. If the federal and state administrations did in fact cut the Medicaid budgets, hospitals faced the prospect that their budgets would be greatly strained as well. If providers voluntarily developed a radical policy alternative that was acceptable to the King administration, all parties might benefit.

Representatives of several of Boston's major teaching hospitals—New England Medical Center, Beth Israel Hospital, and Massachusetts General Hospital—met first to consider organizing a response to this issue. As a result of their initial meeting a larger Medicaid task force was established to examine strategies for controlling Medicaid costs. The group rejected traditional means of cost control: reducing payment rates, cutting eligibility, reducing benefits, or cross-subsidizing through other payers. Instead, the task force proposed that a provider consortium be organized to enroll Boston Medicaid recipients in a managed health care program, with financial incentives for providers to deliver care more efficiently.

In July 1981 a three-year planning grant was awarded to the teaching hospital task force by the Commonwealth Fund of New York to support the formation of the consortium. The Commonwealth Health Care Corporation was established as a formal nonprofit organization in December 1981, and an executive director was hired. At that time both CHCC's membership and its governing board consisted solely of hospitals. Growing concern among the city's neighborhood health centers about the future role of the corporation led to negotiations and, in the spring of 1982, to the inclusion of the health centers in CHCC's membership. The board was restructured to include eleven hospitals, eleven health centers, and two consumer representatives (see table 2).

TABLE 2

CHCC BOARD MEMBERS (PROVIDERS)

Hospitals	Health Centers
Beth Israel	Codman Square
Boston City	Dorchester House
Brigham and Women's	East Boston Neighborhood
Carney	Harvard Street/Charles Drew
Children's Hospital Medical Center	Mattapan
Deaconess	Neponset
Faulkner	South Boston
Massachusetts Eye and Ear	South Cove
Massachusetts General	South End Community
New England Medical Center	Upham's Corner
University	Whittier Street

NOTE: Two consumer representatives were also board members.

21

CHCC initially proposed to provide care for one segment of Boston's Medicaid population: recipients of Aid to Families with Dependent Children (AFDC), some 70,000 mothers and children constituting about 23,000 families. The elderly and disabled poor, also covered by Medicaid, were not included. CHCC would receive from the state a fixed monthly payment for each person covered by AFDC and contract for medical services with its member hospitals, health centers, hospital outpatient departments, and physicians' groups. All AFDC recipients would be allowed to select a site (from among participating providers) at which they preferred to receive care. Once the site was picked, recipients could receive medical services only at that site except in emergencies. All eligible AFDC families would be required to enroll in CHCC.

In design, at least, CHCC served the interests of all parties: hospitals would accept a decline in Medicaid revenue at their expensive outpatient departments in exchange for a better payment rate for CHCC patients requiring hospitalization. Moreover, hospitals would operate under a Medicaid revenue budget on which they could plan well in advance. Health centers could anticipate that additional patients and Medicaid revenues would be directed to them rather than to hospital outpatient departments because CHCC's financial incentives encouraged the use of low-cost primary care sites. The state could look forward to reducing the Medicaid budget by closing the open-ended financing for at least one group of recipients. Because of capitation payments to CHCC, the state could also expect a relatively fixed budget for AFDC recipients. Finally, AFDC recipients who participated could look forward to better continuity of care from health centers and hospitals. The use of physician managers in the program would give many recipients their first ongoing relationship with a physician.

In June 1982 CHCC submitted a program planning document to the Massachusetts Executive Office of Human Services giving a preliminary description of the proposed program. Subsequently, CHCC and the state began a joint planning and development process to elaborate the components of the program further. On September 1, 1982, they signed a memorandum of understanding expressing their intent to move toward negotiating a contract by July 1983.

In anticipation of this contract the state submitted to the federal Health Care Financing Administration (HCFA) a request for the waivers required to implement a managed care program for all Boston Medicaid recipients in the AFDC category. The most important was a waiver of the Medicaid freedom-of-choice provision, since CHCC and the state were exploring the possibility that enrollment in CHCC be mandatory for Boston AFDC recipients. The state's commitment to a waiver of patients' freedom of choice eventually became a major point of dispute. CHCC officials maintain that the state agreed to mandatory enrollment early in the planning process. State officials contend, however, that this issue was always open to negotiation and was to depend on CHCC's ability to provide data and analysis clearly justifying the need; the waiver request was submitted to give the state the *option* of making enrollment mandatory.

As a unique partnership that brought together the public sector, some of the nation's finest teaching hospitals, and the community health centers, CHCC drew national interest and attention. Several private foundations expressed their support for it by providing funds for the development and start-up of the managed care delivery system.

The foundations saw CHCC as an innovative, collaborative solution to increasing Medicaid budget problems, using market incentives rather than regulation. The Robert Wood Johnson Foundation, which committed $1.2 million over three years to design and implement the delivery system, viewed CHCC as the "flagship of its new program to foster prepaid, managed health care for the poor" and proposed to provide $9.6 million to fund similar efforts in other cities. The Hartford Foundation granted CHCC funds to develop quality assurance mechanisms and incentives for physicians that would foster cost-effective clinical decisions. The Blue Cross/Massachusetts Hospital Fund gave CHCC a grant to design a payment system incorporating incentives and risks for participating providers.

Components of the Program

The idea underlying CHCC is that significant savings in any state Medicaid program can be accomplished by combining two elements: (1) efficiency in the clinical management of patient care through continuity of care and coordination of medical services by providers, and (2) reordered economic incentives for providers to promote such savings. That is, CHCC planned to restructure the delivery system to encourage existing providers, traditionally paid on a fee-for-service basis, to act like health maintenance organizations (HMOs): to accept a fixed payment per patient, with potential financial rewards for efficient behavior and financial losses for inefficient behavior.

Five components needed to be developed: (1) the managed care delivery system, (2) a payment system with financial incentives for cost-effective care, (3) a program for education and enrollment of patients, (4) a quality assurance plan, and (5) a sophisticated com-

23

puterized management information system (MIS).

Under the managed care system, existing providers would organize themselves into health plans called COREs (coordinated operating and reporting entities). A recipient enrolling in the CHCC program would choose a specific CORE and a primary care physician who would serve as the manager for all medical care provided to that enrollee. The physician manager would be responsible for

- providing health maintenance care
- requesting return visits
- ordering/coordinating ancillary services
- making referrals
- determining need/referring for hospitalization
- determining need/coordinating home care, long-term care, and rehabilitation services

Health care facilities eligible to become COREs included hospital outpatient departments, health centers, HMOs, private physicians and group practices, and any combination of these (see figure 2). Each CORE would be required to deliver or contract for basic health care services, including twenty-four-hour on-call services for pediatrics, internal medicine, obstetrics and gynecology, laboratory, and hospital referrals. Other services, such as mental health, dental care, pharmacy, and social services, were the subject of intense discussion; whether COREs would provide them under their capitation payment or contract for them on a fee-for-service basis outside the CHCC structure was not resolved.

The central corporate functions of CHCC were to administer the program and the COREs and to design and implement a payment system incorporating financial incentives and risks to encourage cost-effective management of patients' care. The corporation would receive fixed monthly payments per enrollee from the state and would pay each CORE a per capita sum for its enrolled population, putting the CORE at risk for costs greater than that amount.

The design included developing policies and procedures for enrolling AFDC recipients in the CORE health plans. Although CHCC proposed that enrollment be mandatory for all 70,000 Boston AFDC recipients, it was considered crucial to allow recipients their choice of CORE and the ability to maintain existing relationships with physicians if they desired. To educate and enroll this number of recipients effectively in coordination with existing state systems and procedures was an immense logistical task.

Because a prepaid program and its incentives to contain costs may lead providers to reduce the quality of care, CHCC also proposed

FIGURE 2

CORE CONFIGURATIONS AND POSSIBLE VARIATIONS WITHIN MODELS

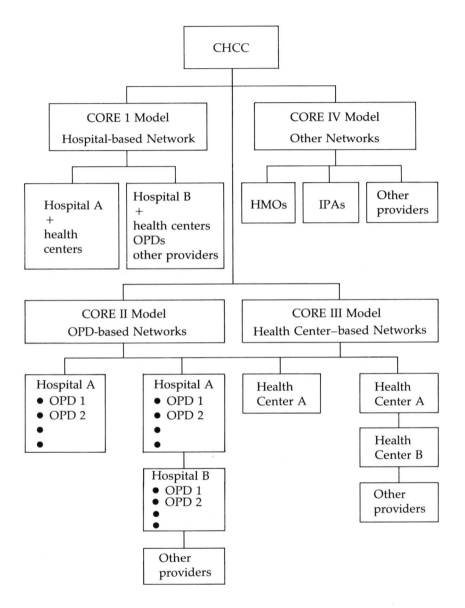

NOTE: HMO = health maintenance organization; IPA = individual practice association; OPD = outpatient department.

to institute formal quality assurance programs at two levels. Each CORE would be required to establish a medical review program to monitor the quality of care provided to its enrollees, and CHCC would carry out its own central quality assurance review.

Another key to the success of the program was a sophisticated management information system MIS to monitor providers' accountability, utilization, and financial incentives, as well as to carry out claims processing and corroboration of AFDC eligibility. The MIS was to have modules for enrollment/eligibility checking, utilization/claims processing, financial administration, and planning/budgeting. Although the MIS requirements were technically demanding, this aspect of the program was perhaps the easiest to develop; the systems were expensive, but expertise was available, and no politics were involved.

The Development Phase

In January 1983, with money from the Robert Wood Johnson Foundation grant, program development began in earnest. The full complement of CHCC corporate staff was hired, including a director of finance, a director of operations, four CORE operations managers, and several analysts. CHCC was unable to find a medical director, however, and this plagued its credibility in the area of quality assurance during the months to come.

Plans for CORE networks, quality assurance programs, and operational protocols were elaborated in consultation with provider members. An MIS vendor contract was signed; and models of the payment system were proposed for discussion by providers. With regular consultation with the staff of the Massachusetts Department of Public Welfare (the state Medicaid authority), the CHCC staff began to develop educational materials and enrollment procedures for AFDC recipients. Work plans were oriented toward signing a formal state contract in the summer of 1983 and implementing the program in late fall that year (see figure 3).

During this period the state submitted its waiver requests to HCFA and received waivers for CHCC of federal regulations governing the Medicaid program. The regulations waived included freedom of choice of provider and the requirement that at least 25 percent of the clients of prepaid health plans enrolling Medicaid recipients be non-Medicaid clients.[1] State legislation was filed to exempt CHCC from regulation by the Massachusetts Division of Insurance, which governs prepaid health plans. This exemption would have allowed CHCC to administer public funds without public regulation.

During the development phase, CHCC also identified several

FIGURE 3

Proposed Flow of Planning Activities during CHCC's
Development Phase,
September 1982–July 1983

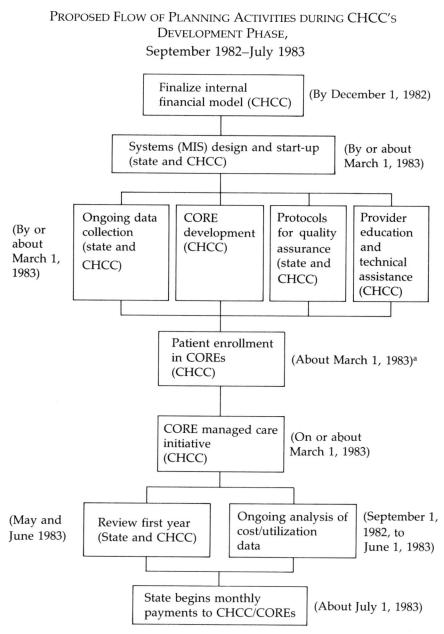

a. Enrollment and CORE managed care delivery not to begin until a formal contract between CHCC and the state had been negotiated.   Payment would   continue on a fee-for-service basis for the first four months after implementation.

constituencies, which coalesced around common interests. The hospitals and health centers were one constituency (or perhaps two, since hospitals and health centers often had different concerns). This group was most important in the negotiation of a financial model. CHCC had been organized in response to the threat of arbitrary cuts in Medicaid reimbursement, and its member organizations had a common interest in developing a program under their own control to avoid those cuts. The CHCC payment system would constitute a significant change and include financial risk as a fundamental incentive.

Community advocacy groups were another constituency. Although they were not formally involved in the planning process, they were extremely concerned about a mandatory health care program for Boston AFDC recipients and fundamentally mistrustful of its focus on teaching hospitals. Since the program had been initiated because of its potential ability to cut Medicaid spending, welfare advocacy groups were concerned that costs might be cut at the expense of quality.

Physicians were viewed as a separate constituency from the hospitals' and health centers' administrative staffs. Since the heart of the managed care concept was cost-effective management by the primary care physician, it was crucial to teach physicians about this role and arouse their interest in it. Without their commitment, the program could not be successfully implemented or effective in achieving its goal.

Finally, the state administration was a constituency with several concerns. These included the potential savings of the program and its capacity to provide high-quality care.

Factors Leading to Dissolution

Most aspects of CHCC's development phase appeared smooth on the surface, or at least manageable. A number of factors were beginning to coalesce, however, that would lead to the eventual dissolution, rather than implementation, of CHCC. The most dramatic and readily identifiable factor was the unexpected change of administration in Massachusetts. In January 1983 Michael Dukakis took office as governor, having received substantial support from a liberal coalition in the election. The concerns of welfare advocacy groups and supporters of a bigger public sector had a more receptive audience than under the King administration, and the desirability of a private sector response to a public sector budget problem became more questionable.

Moreover, the CHCC initiative was beginning to lose credibility. A review of state and CHCC documents exchanged during the last months of 1982, as well as discussions with key persons involved with the program, shows a mounting concern on the part of many state officials and public and provider constituencies that aspects of CHCC's design were flawed and that CHCC was taking too long to show in detail how it intended to accomplish its mission. Many of the specific concerns can be grouped under two large issues, addressed in detail below. First, was CHCC going to save the state money and, if so, how and how much? Second, what was the justification for removing Medicaid recipients' freedom to choose among health care providers? Cutting across both these issues was the significance of changes in the state administration and resultant changes in the relationship between CHCC and the state.

Costs. The CHCC could never articulate a firm price for the proposed program, in part because the state government lacked the data on costs and use to corroborate exactly how Medicaid money is spent. As a result, negotiations with providers over an acceptable capitation rate proved nearly impossible. The absence of cost projections was a major shortcoming from the outset but seemed to draw greater criticism from the Dukakis administration. In CHCC's defense, Massachusetts did not initiate a computerized Medicaid management information system (MMIS) until 1983. The MMIS enabled health planners to determine for the first time from historical data how often Medicaid clients were likely to visit doctors for various ailments, how often and how long they were likely to be hospitalized, which tests were likely to be ordered by physicians, and so on. Without such data during CHCC's development phase, it was impossible to determine accurately how much medical care 70,000 AFDC recipients were likely to require annually, from what types of providers (health centers, hospitals, specialty hospitals), and at what cost (total and per capita).

Using money from its Blue Cross grant, CHCC attempted to collect cost and utilization data site by site from its member hospitals and health centers. This was a mammoth task because many providers still do not have computerized records of such data. Moreover, since much of the information was being collected centrally for the first time and would be revealed to the state (and other providers) for planning in the absence of a firm contract, hospital members of the consortium were especially reluctant to share publicly data on their costs and revenues. CHCC staff members were placed in the difficult position of middlemen—needing to share financial data with the state for planning purposes but also feeling loyal to the interest of CHCC's members.

In the absence of good information, discussions among providers of an acceptable financial model were labored and unproductive. Without historical cost and utilization data to assess the risk they would be assuming under a capitation payment system and to determine the changes needed for financially sound performance, providers were reluctant to commit themselves to a payment system incorporating significant financial risk. In addition, some hospitals were concerned about covering certain so-called noncomparable costs, primarily those associated with teaching. Moreover, the health centers argued that implementing managed care systems in their facilities would entail large start-up costs that should be paid by CHCC; they also maintained that managed care might increase their unit costs of providing routine primary care and that the increased costs should be reflected in the capitation rate.

The absence of reliable and valid historical data on Medicaid utilization rates and costs, coupled with the diverse financial concerns and cost structures of CHCC's provider members, made the development of a financial plan for the program tedious. If the program had become effective in 1983–1984, the state would have paid CHCC a sum of money equal to Medicaid expenditures incurred in 1982 plus inflation. Expenditures for AFDC eligibles are about 30 percent of the state's total Medicaid budget—$66 million for Boston.

The initial payment model called for funds to be divided into two accounts—one for inpatient hospital bills and one for outpatient care. The inpatient fund would pay hospital bills on a fee-for-service basis, an arrangement that caused many critics to argue that CHCC offered no incentive to decrease the price of inpatient hospital care, which is a major contributor to the inflation of medical costs. As one state official pointed out, "CHCC would only have been able to save money on hospital costs by reducing the amount of inpatient services through prior approval and careful case management. This would put inordinate pressure on case manager physicians to control use of hospital facilities." Some critics feared the result would be clinically dangerous and ethically unsound medical practice.

The outpatient fund would have covered all health care services provided in ambulatory settings. Each CORE would have received a fixed budget based on its enrolled population. The budget for hospital-based COREs would have been adjusted upward for a "hospital overhead factor." One person interviewed considered this adjustment a "fudge factor designed to cover the higher costs of teaching programs and hospital overhead. The fudge factor therefore reduced incentives for hospital-based COREs to reduce their costs or shift care out of hospital outpatient departments into less costly settings." Even if use of services had been substantially decreased, some of those interviewed believed, CHCC would have achieved only moderate savings, perhaps not even enough to cover its proposed administrative costs of $3.3 million per year.[2]

Another budgetary issue often mentioned during our interviews was CHCC's decision to enroll only AFDC families, which are the least expensive segment of the Medicaid population to treat. For the most part, AFDC recipients are healthy women and children who need routine adult, obstetric, and pediatric care. Only 30 percent of the state's Medicaid budget is spent on AFDC families even though they make up 70 percent of the Medicaid population. As one state official pointed out, "It is the non-AFDC population that is by far the greatest financial burden on the state. Not applying managed care techniques to this population will result in little if any financial advantage to the state from the CHCC plan." Proponents of CHCC argue, however, that "the AFDC population was the logical place to start. CHCC was going to be complicated enough; why not begin with the population that places the fewest demands on the health care system?" Moreover, since AFDC families have the fewest and weakest ties to independent private physicians, any disruption caused by the changeover to CHCC would have been minimized.

As a compromise, CHCC proposed a contract that would immediately have referred patients to CHCC centers and hospitals but would have retained a fee-for-service reimbursement system for one year until data on costs and use could be generated and a realistic budget proposed. The state was reluctant to accept this proposal. The Dukakis administration wanted to realize savings quickly; otherwise, it could see little point in undertaking the administrative risks posed by CHCC. The state therefore urged CHCC to provide detailed cost projections (even if they were only estimates) and plans showing how managed care systems, as implemented by the COREs, would change the behavior of providers and Medicaid recipients. The latter are historically heavy users of expensive hospital emergency rooms and often consult several physicians for the same ailment, generating repetitive diagnostic testing and treatment costs.

By most accounts, CHCC's responses to the state's requests for information were vague and unsatisfactory. Members of the King administration had been sympathetic to CHCC's problems of poor or nonexistent data and also recognized its unwillingness to offer rough estimates that might become the basis for negotiations despite the possibility of major inaccuracies. The Dukakis administration, however, grew increasingly impatient. It felt that the program was being railroaded through with poor planning and that the teaching hospitals were attempting to use CHCC to get the highest possible Medicaid payment rates with the lowest assumed risk. One critic raised the issue of the hospitals' "less-than-exemplary record of controlling costs" and questioned both the need for an intermediary such as CHCC to stand between the state government and health care providers and the wisdom of such an arrangement. Other critics voiced concern about the disturbing lack of proposed regulation for CHCC. Among welfare rights advocates, standards for quality of care were a major concern because enrollment in CHCC would be mandatory. They argued that the capitation payment viewed by CHCC planners as an incentive for efficiency was an inducement to providers to lower the quality of care.

Freedom of Choice. All those we interviewed and the majority of secondary accounts describing the collapse of CHCC agreed that if CHCC foundered on a single issue, that issue was the freedom of Medicaid recipients to participate only if they chose. Freedom of choice was the cornerstone of the 1966 Medicaid act, which was intended to abolish a two-class system of medical care by giving low-income persons equal access to the health system. The 1981 Omnibus Budget Reconciliation Act allowed the Department of Health and Human Services for the first time to waive freedom of choice to encourage experimental state programs designed to reform the Medicaid program and reduce its costs. The Massachusetts waiver application in support of the CHCC initiative included a waiver of freedom of choice. The application was submitted, however, by the King administration, whose philosophy was more closely aligned with the Reagan administration's policies than was that of the Dukakis administration. Although Governor King's staff was never fully committed to a mandatory program, the Dukakis administration immediately gave closer and more skeptical consideration to the issue.

CHCC deemed voluntary enrollment unacceptable, and its staff and planning documents clearly stated why the need for a large "critical mass" of enrollees was seen as crucial to the program's viability. First, if CHCC was to be a highly centralized management program acting as an intermediary between the state and multiple provider networks, it would be administratively expensive, requiring a sizable number of enrollees to carry the overhead costs. The justification for such an expensive program was that only sophisticated oversight mechanisms could generate the savings promised to the state and spread the financial risk implicit in a fixed capitation contract. Perhaps less explicitly stated was the belief of CHCC officials that the Massachusetts Medicaid program staff could not be relied on for the kind of detailed, timely feedback on use and costs that would prove crucial to CHCC's success; CHCC would need to develop and maintain its own computer systems, management procedures, and procedures for checking eligibility for Medicaid.

CHCC's planning staff also argued that, given the demographics of the AFDC population, a substantial enrollment was necessary to induce changes in providers' behavior. If CHCC was to achieve its desired economies of scale and participating hospitals were to be given enough incentive to alter their financial behavior, virtually all of Boston's AFDC recipients were needed. Although Boston's AFDC population constitutes 20 percent of the statewide total, it accounts for only a small fraction of the ambulatory care volume among the city's medical care providers—18 percent of the health care visits and 11 percent of the hospital ambulatory visits, according to the CHCC. To have any influence on providers' clinical decisions, the CHCC staff reasoned, a majority of those visits—preferably 100 percent—would have to be under CHCC auspices. The staff believed that 70,000 AFDC recipients could not be enticed to join the program through traditional marketing mechanisms and voluntary enrollment. Mandatory enrollment seemed the only way.

The King administration had threatened to reduce the Medicaid rolls by thousands of people and cut benefits dramatically for those who remained eligible. When CHCC was initiated, mandatory enrollment in a managed care system seemed a far less offensive solution and in keeping with federal interests. But by late 1982 the budgetary crisis in Massachusetts had eased. In fact, the legislature did not pass Governor King's proposal to cut the Medicaid budget by 25 percent, choosing instead to enact a new set of controls on hospital budgets that promised savings to the state far greater than CHCC could hope to achieve.

CHCC's executive director and board knew that they would encounter some opposition to mandatory enrollment under the new administration but assumed that it would largely be overcome for these reasons: since CHCC's provider consortium included (or had invited to participate) virtually all the health care providers in Boston, it really did not restrict freedom of choice; CHCC had received national attention and massive financial support; and the state had already obtained the needed federal waivers. As one CHCC official said, "It was more or less assumed that there was not much question about mandatory enrollment. We just assumed that we'd do it. And, unlike the California of Ronald Reagan, it was not a question of somebody developing an overnight plan and a whole bunch of entrepreneurs arriving in polyester suits." None of the CHCC staff or administration recognized how extensively plans for the program would be affected by the Dukakis administration, in part because the new governor seemed receptive to innovation. It also took him some months to assemble the human services team that would continue the negotiations started by King appointees.

State officials acknowledge that they were silent for a long time on the CHCC issue, although from the beginning the Dukakis administration made clear its extreme concern over the fears expressed by welfare rights advocates. The administration was also not enthusiastic about giving greater latitude to the private sector to manage welfare programs. In February 1983 CHCC made its major presentation to Dukakis's secretary of human services, who was very interested in the timetable for implementing CHCC. Because Governor Dukakis had not yet appointed a new welfare commissioner, the current Medicaid director had ceased substantive negotiations with CHCC. In April, however, he sent the secretary of human services a memorandum pointing out the growing opposition to mandatory enrollment and urging the secretary to "make a clear choice between a system based on mandatory enrollment and one that is predicated on voluntary incentive-based enrollment."

By the spring of 1983 it was obvious that the secretary would not support mandatory enrollment in CHCC. To make matters worse for the consortium, some of the health center directors began to be criticized by their own boards. One center director has stated that many health centers opposed mandatory enrollment all along.

On July 6, 1983, CHCC offered the state its "minimum necessary criteria" for a viable program: it proposed to establish a year-long managed care project on a fee-for-service basis at first, moving to capitation in the second year. It would need to enroll 34,000–40,000 people to break even, and the state would have to develop adequate incentives and marketing efforts to guarantee "the minimum enrollment level within a reasonable time period." CHCC also offered its best estimate—6 percent—of potential reductions in medical costs during the initial period of operation. The state would not share in any savings until that 6 percent threshold was exceeded. State officials refused, claiming that it was impossible to guarantee enrollment in a voluntary program. They also determined that it was not in the best public interest to incur large incentive and marketing costs for CHCC, obtain no savings, and be expected to defray the possible administrative funding shortfall.

The state submitted a letter to CHCC recommending three possible options: (1) implement a smaller-scale managed care program; (2) continue planning for another year and provide better data and justification; or (3) reorient the program completely to take on managed care for the elderly or some other subgroup of the Medicaid population. These suggestions proved unacceptable to CHCC, and on July 29, 1983, its board of directors decided to abandon all further plans for the program. A week later the new state welfare commissioner was notified that the CHCC board had decided to terminate the program.

It is difficult to assign the responsibility for the decision to one party. In some ways the decision reflected an internal consensus that a program of managed care for all Boston Medicaid recipients was an idea whose time had not yet arrived, or had come and gone. Many CHCC representatives feel in retrospect that the decision to dismantle the program was made externally and forced on them by public pressure and state unresponsiveness.

With the change of administration, the state was increasingly receptive to the growing concern about mandatory enrollment. Even before the state had explicitly stated this concern, however, provider members of CHCC became aware that the program they were planning was exceedingly unpopular among some community groups. Neighborhood health centers, which had always been the champions of community concerns, found themselves promoting an idea that was vehemently opposed by some of their customary allies.

We conclude that CHCC started as an innovative response to a state initiative to cut costs. After the election its image underwent a slow metamorphosis, and it came to be seen as an unpopular, self-serving providers' initiative. Somehow, through changes in the external environment, support for the program was substantially eroded. CHCC's inability or unwillingness to provide explicit information on its projected costs and cost savings made it difficult to overcome waning state support. More important, by the time the administration changed, it was too late for CHCC to build a strong base of public support among the AFDC population and welfare rights advocates.

The three alternatives proposed by the state essentially meant the end of the original concept, which was to be an overall structural change in the provision of services to Medicaid recipients. Funding was not available for an open-ended planning process, and a scaled-down focus for CHCC, though a commendable suggestion, was fundamentally different from the program conceived by Boston's health care providers.

A Perspective on the Program's Demise

The response to CHCC's demise has been mixed. State officials argue that CHCC was not a good pilot for an experimental Medicaid program because it was more a command-and-control than a true incentive system. Welfare rights activists in the state view the decision to terminate CHCC as "real good news" and point out that the program was terminated because of the charges that it was trying to force poor people into a managed health program. Some observers view CHCC as a "genuine effort by hospitals to gain control over a shrinking Medicaid fund." Others argue that CHCC was an excellent idea that was sabotaged by the Dukakis administration in its unwillingness to alienate vocal constituents of its governing coalition.

We have tried to show that the causes of CHCC's failure were varied and complex. First, it was in part a failure to communicate CHCC's goals to its major—but most overlooked—constituency, Medicaid recipients. Having been directly involved in the planning of the CHCC program, we have been continually surprised and dismayed by the misinformation about it that has appeared in print: about its operations, its plans for quality assurance, and the issue of freedom of choice. Clearly, its administration did not communicate effectively about the program to the people whom it wanted to enroll. This failure was due to factors endogenous to CHCC.

Poor communication with the public, especially welfare recipients, eventually became CHCC's greatest handicap. The impartial observer can see, for example, that because CHCC proposed to include all providers in the city, some freedom of choice could have been maintained.[3] But this was never made clear to the proposed participants. Perhaps one of the major lessons to be learned from CHCC is the importance to Medicaid initiatives of being supported by consumers. Strong consumer advocacy for the program might have helped overcome issues of enrollment, political support, image, and poor data.

Factors exogenous to CHCC include changes in the environment. The crisis that originally enticed private and public sectors to come together abated so quickly that by the 1982 elections a political commitment to a private sector solution had diminished. The trade-offs and compromises inherent in the freedom of choice issue would probably have been made willingly by the state if a perceived crisis had existed. A major question that merits further study is whether a CHCC-style initiative works under certain environmental and political conditions but is not a broadly applicable solution to the problem of Medicaid cost escalation.

The different assumptions and perceptions that CHCC and the Dukakis administration brought to the final negotiating session were also important. For providers, CHCC was a "grand mission" to bring the Boston medical community together in a noble experiment. (Although there was altruism in CHCC's approach, Boston's providers also enjoyed the prestige and national attention they were attracting for their innovative efforts to contain Medicaid costs.) CHCC officials believe that the state viewed the program too narrowly—seeing it only as a cost-containment initiative and not as a chance for a "great experiment" in restructuring the health delivery system through public and private sector cooperation: "The state said that because it [CHCC] would not save enough money it was not worth doing. But we had everyone at the table who had the power to make the necessary political compromises to change health care delivery in Boston."

The statements by CHCC's officials seem to ignore the tremendous credibility gap facing hospitals, which have long been perceived as major obstacles to cost control. In asking the state government to turn over to them a large share of public funds, on faith and with very few solid answers, providers aroused more than a little suspicion in the public and state officials. CHCC's unresponsiveness to proposed reductions in the scope of the program did not help this image. Many state officials interviewed for this case study felt that the scope of the program and the chance for national attention were all that mattered to CHCC and that, if there had been a true desire to help reduce costs and change delivery, "they wouldn't have taken their marbles and gone home because the game would not be played entirely by their rules."

Another frequently articulated position was that CHCC should not have given up because of the mandatory enrollment issue. The state offered CHCC a number of options: scale down the project to a demonstration; spend another year in planning; redirect attention to the elderly. The Robert Wood Johnson Foundation would have funded additional planning to enable CHCC to redirect itself, and state staff members admit that they would ultimately have been more receptive to a large-scale program if CHCC had been able to offer some proof—based on a preliminary scaled-down operation—that it would work. CHCC offered convincing reasons why the program had to be all or nothing; it is fair to ask, however, whether there was some reluctance on the part of its members to have to prove themselves.

State officials also point out that CHCC never evolved past a concept for providing care into an actual program; that the initial plans, though good, were never further developed or well documented to constitute a real product for the state to purchase. Staff members of the Department of Public Welfare claim that they never received from CHCC data showing what its effects would be or projections of cost savings. They ask how the state could justify pouring nearly $70 million into a program that could not be clearly or concretely defined. CHCC staff members point out that they were dependent on the state's history with Medicaid patients to project their own program costs. The inability of the state to provide good planning data and CHCC's reluctance to share preliminary projections with the state in the absence of concrete information created a Catch-22 situation that thwarted the negotiating process from the inception of the development phase. Clearly, it was impossible to negotiate a program of the size and complexity of CHCC without good planning data.

An additional question that must be raised is whether the program had conflicting goals, with no clear-cut priorities that the organization was willing to pursue at the expense of other concerns. CHCC's records reveal a clear picture of an organization struggling to present a plan that met state cost-containment objectives while at the same time attempting to hold together a fragile coalition of providers by making all its members happy. Unfortunately, not all providers can be "kept whole" under stringent efforts to reduce costs. In an attempt to meet the financial interests of all its members, CHCC was ultimately unable to adopt a payment system. Its correspondence with the state reflects its dual objectives. In the view of one state official, each new submission raised "20 new questions which could not be answered and made CHCC appear even more nebulous. It was impossible for the state to move towards a viable negotiating process when CHCC did not represent a compromise between state and provider interests."

The state ultimately viewed CHCC only as a potential vendor with a poorly defined product to sell. "Make or buy" is a phrase used to refer to services that are either provided directly by the state or contracted out. We conclude that the state of Massachusetts was very interested in purchasing a public service of the size and scope of CHCC but that the product for sale was not clearly specified. As the secretary of human services stated, "You had damn well better have a good, tight, clean, clear product. That's what was missing."

The absence of data for detailed program documentation and of a supportive local constituency that had influence with the new administration proved stronger than CHCC's national reputation or the potential embarrassment to the state of a collapse of the entire collaborative effort. Our analysis suggests that CHCC was ultimately a "political animal," dependent on a receptive audience and a prevailing policy perspective favoring private sector alternatives to public sector problems, the use of market incentives, and self-regulation by providers of medical care. As we stated earlier, however, it is unclear whether these conditions are required for all Medicaid cost-containment experiments. It may be that either of two conditions can be met: If a Medicaid initiative can offer (and disseminate to its constituencies) clear, quantitatively documented justification that it offers a better cost and quality alternative to existing public programs, there seems to be nothing that would preclude that program from transcending an unfavorable political climate or interest group politics. Conversely, in a politically supportive environment, a program may not need to offer detailed documentation to justify its implementation.

Our analysis of CHCC indicates certain characteristics that are critical for the implementation and ultimate success of Medicaid cost-containment initiatives:

- Good data must be available for planning purposes.
- The program must be well documented, operationally and financially.
- All important constituencies must be carefully identified early in the planning process.
- Clearly worded explanatory materials about the program must be disseminated to all identified constituencies and directed to their interests and concerns.
- The program must strive for support from consumers, regardless of its initial impetus.

Bibliography

In addition to reviewing CHCC planning documents, state planning documents, and correspondence between CHCC and the state, we used the following materials in the preparation of this case study.

Brooks, Warren. "Duke Scuttles New Health Program." *Boston Globe*, August 2, 1983.

Carballo, Manuel. Letter to the Editor. "CHCC—A Well-intended Response That Didn't Work." *Boston Globe*, August 11, 1983.

CHCC. *Program Planning Document to Develop a Managed Care Initiative for the AFDC Population in Boston.* November 1982.

Hooley, James. "Health Plan That Grew Out of Caring." *Boston Globe*, August 16, 1983.

Knox, Richard. "Commonwealth Health Care Corporation: Bad News for Medicaid Recipients." *Staying Alive* (a publication of Common Health, no. 8), May 1983.

————. "Prepaid Medicaid Experiment Collapses in Massachusetts." *AMA News*, September 9, 1983, p. 3.

Loth, Renee. "Bottom-Line Health: Giving AFDC Folks the Treatment." *Boston Phoenix*, February 9, 1983.

Notes

1. Waiver of freedom of choice was available as the result of the Omnibus Reconciliation Act, which sought to create conditions suitable to state cost-containment experiments; the 25 percent non-Medicaid provision was waived under the justification that CHCC's provider members were primarily non-Medicaid.

2. About 5 percent of the total AFDC Medicaid budget.

3. All existing HMOs and individual practice associations (IPAs) were invited to participate, and group practices and solo practitioners could become CORE sites.

3

The Hospital Payment System in Massachusetts

Susan R. Windham and Paula Griswold

Introduction

This case study examines Chapter 372 of the Acts of 1982, relating to the regulation of hospital revenues and charges in the Commonwealth of Massachusetts. The purpose of the case study is twofold: first, to analyze the substance of the Chapter 372 legislation (the *content* of the law) and second, to examine the coalition approach to negotiation of this regulatory system (the development *process*).

Chapter 372 was enacted by the Massachusetts legislature on August 3, 1982, and signed one week later by then-Governor Edward J. King. The new hospital financing system resulted from a two-year negotiation process that included payers, providers, and regulators of hospital-related services in the commonwealth. Chapter 372 establishes an annual budget for each hospital and, regardless of actual hospital costs, guarantees revenues to meet that budget. The payment system is prospective and includes incentives for cost control and for reducing unnecessary use of health care services. The burden to operate within the fixed budget rests with each hospital. No parallel incentives exist for physicians, who make most decisions about resource allocation within a hospital. Similar to the Medicare DRG payment system, hospitals that treat patients for less than the predetermined "price" retain the difference. Conversely, if expenses exceed fixed revenues, hospitals lose money.

As the state's first global hospital budgeting system, Chapter 372 has been closely scrutinized. Some observers suggest that Chapter 372 irrevocably locks Massachusetts into a "public utility" financing model, rewarding politically powerful institutions, stifling price competition among hospitals, and acting as a barrier to the market for new delivery and financing alternatives. Yet HMOs, which are proliferating rapidly in Massachusetts, are guaranteed the right to contract with hospitals for medical services at or below prevailing prices. Also, PPOs are negotiating discounts with hospitals, although disagreement lingers among system designers on Chapter 372's intent in this area.

Others, especially members of the provider community, believe that the payment system precipitates a decline in both quality and innovation, shifting the focus of preeminent medical treatment, research, and education from Massachusetts to other parts of the country. Some even suggest that Chapter 372 discourages continued growth of medical technology-related businesses, which have burgeoned in Massachusetts over the past decade, contributing to the strength of the state's economy.

Business and industry in general take a different view, arguing that the status quo in Massachusetts was unacceptable and that Chapter 372 will produce long-run benefits. An assessment of the state's economic climate by the Massachusetts Business Roundtable concluded that "Careful study of the regulations and incentives which drive the health care business clearly indicates that the system is not structured to respond in a competitive, efficient manner to the demand of consumers for medical care. Government has reacted to cost increases with often contradictory regulatory strategies which appear to foster system growth and inhibit competition."[1]

The balance of this case study reviews the environment in Massachusetts that preceded Chapter 372; briefly highlights events that led to its passage; outlines basic elements of the legislation; reviews its early impact; and explores, especially from the business community's perspective, some of its strengths and weaknesses as an incremental step toward long-term health care cost control.

The Health Care Environment in Massachusetts

Massachusetts has long been identified with medical education, research, and technological development. In Boston alone over a dozen tertiary-care teaching hospitals house training and research activities for the medical schools of three major universities: Boston, Harvard, and Tufts. A fourth medical school was opened several years ago in Worcester, Massachusetts (about forty miles southwest of Boston), by the University of Massachusetts, and a new teaching hospital was built to support patient care, research, and educational activities. In addition, over 100 acute-care hospitals provide access to high-quality health care in the state's urban and rural areas.

This high standard of medical care has not been earned without paying a price. According to a recent study by the Massachusetts

Business Roundtable ("Health Care Costs in Massachusetts," May 1982), from 1973 through 1980 per capita health expenditures in the commonwealth were 30 percent above the national average. The average cost per hospital stay in Massachusetts was $2,374 in 1979, 45 percent above the national average and the highest in the country. In the late 1970s the number of physicians per capita in Massachusetts was 43 percent above the national average. State and local health-planning agencies contend that Massachusetts is "overbedded," with 2,000–3,500 excess beds. From 1980 through 1982, however, hospitals requested almost one billion dollars through the determination of need (DON) process (Massachusetts' version of Certificate of Need) to finance capital replacement and expansion.

Before the enactment of Chapter 372, hospitals in Massachusetts were reimbursed differently by each of the four major payers—Medicare, Medicaid, Blue Cross, and commercial carriers. Medicare paid costs that it determined were associated with treatment of its patients. Medicaid reimbursed hospitals according to an average per diem rate. Medicare and Medicaid thus provided little incentive for hospitals to treat patients efficiently because revenues were directly linked to expenses. Medicare and Medicaid definitions of costs also did not include many expenses routinely incurred by hospitals, notably bad debt and free care, thereby creating shortfalls that were shifted to private payers.

Prior to 1981 Blue Cross reimbursed Massachusetts hospitals through a contractual agreement, periodically renegotiated. These hospital contracts were basically retrospective, cost-based systems. Blue Cross customers, about two-thirds of the private insurance market in Massachusetts, enjoyed a "discount" on charges paid by commercially insured and private-paying patients. In 1981 this discount was estimated to be about 10.4 percent. The differential in payments between Blue Cross and other private payers fluctuated in part based on the amount of underpayments to hospitals by Medicare and Medicaid, about 10 percent and 20 percent of full costs respectively. In essence, commercially insured patients faced a pricing structure that required them to pay all hospital-incurred costs not covered by other payers. Those costs covered by Blue Cross were partially sheltered from the cost shift, under terms of the prevailing hospital contract.

The Massachusetts Rate Setting Commission monitored this system, reviewing hospital budgets and establishing Medicaid per diems and charges paid by commercially insured and self-pay patients. Hospitals spent enormous amounts of time and resources addressing the commission's potpourri of compliance-oriented regulatory systems in an effort to maximize revenues. Simply put, hospitals had huge financial incentives to manipulate the various payment rules to generate the greatest possible return. Although surpluses or profit margins for the industry were close to zero in the years preceding Chapter 372, cost-based payment virtually guaranteed each institution's fiscal well-being.

Events Leading to Chapter 372. In 1980 regulatory disagreements between hospitals and the Massachusetts Rate Setting Commission escalated as the commission proposed tight new rules on volume as well as on price controls. In lieu of regulations, a short-term limit on revenue increases was passed by the Massachusetts legislature, capping the system while a special commission studied alternative, prospective payment systems for future implementation. Four business representatives were selected to serve on the Joint Legislative–Executive Commission, joined by principals from the hospital industry, Blue Cross of Massachusetts, commercial insurers, the physician community, labor, the Massachusetts legislature, Medicare, Medicaid, and the Rate Setting Commission.

The Joint Legislative-Executive Commission was an excellent forum for businesses to become both knowledgeable about and directly involved in health care policy issues. The commission had top-level representation from each constituency, and its mandate was consistent with business interests in stronger health care cost controls.

Business representatives on the commission included two corporate CEOs and two senior managers, each from a member company of the Massachusetts Business Roundtable. The Massachusetts Business Roundtable (MBR) is an association of the chief executives from nearly every major bank, utility, high-technology, insurance, and manufacturing company in Massachusetts. Together, MBR members employ over 360,000 people. It is interesting to note that the initial list of recommended business appointees to the Joint Commission had to be rejected because every nominee was either a hospital trustee or a director of an insurance company.

In the summer of 1981, while the commission was active, Blue Cross and the Massachusetts Hospital Association agreed to a new type of contract, after the Rate Setting Commission rejected their initial proposal to continue cost-based reimbursement. The new contract, Hospital Agreement–29 (HA–29) established a prospective payment system in which Blue Cross revenues were set in advance for each hospital and were predictable over a three-year term. As "quid pro quos" for guaranteed revenues, hospitals agreed for the first time to accept financial risk, assuming responsibility for costs in excess of Blue Cross's maximum allowable costs (MAC).

Incentives under HA–29 were structured to encourage more efficient use of inpatient and outpatient hospital resources. HA–29 financed only about 25 percent of a hospital's patients, on average. Medicare and Medicaid remained cost-based payers, and the balance of private patients paid charges.

HA–29 was studied extensively by the Joint Legislative-Executive Commission as it developed its recommendations for reform of the payment system. In its Study Report dated November 2, 1981, the commission set forth seventeen major issues it felt should be considered in an effort to revise the hospital reimbursement system:

- prospective orientation
- affordable expenditure limits
- inclusion of all payers and hospitals
- elimination of cross-subsidies
- equitable allocation of bad debt and charity care
- equitable allocation of payment shortfalls
- predictability and stability
- consistent definition of hospital financial requirements
- incentives for efficiency and productivity
- regulatory efficiencies such as uniform audit, review, and reporting requirements
- appropriate hospital inflation factors
- utilization review
- system's effect on the functioning of alternative delivery systems
- linkages to health planning
- ongoing performance evaluation
- independent administering body
- adequate time for implementation

By Spring 1982, discussion in the Joint Legislative-Executive Commission was stalled, and efforts to agree on legislation had deteriorated. The only active legislative option was a bill (S.495) defining a uniform payment system, introduced by the Massachusetts Senate majority leader and strongly supported by the commercial industry. Proponents pushed S.495 as an extension of the concepts of the HA–29 contract to all payers. Blue Cross and Massachusetts Hospital Association representatives on the commission strongly opposed the bill. Deadlocked, the commission voted to adjourn.

In May MBR's board voted to support a revised version of S.495 despite the threat of higher costs in the short run for almost half of its membership (the Blue Cross accounts). The Roundtable board also directed the chairman of its Health Care Task Force to attempt to broker a compromise among a coalition of representatives from the Massachusetts Hospital Association, Medicaid, the Rate Setting Commission, Blue Cross, and the commercial insurance industry's policy group, the Life Insurance Association of Massachusetts.

Initially planned as a ten-day, "last-ditch" effort, these negotiations continued until late June 1982 when hospital representatives withdrew, unwilling to join other coalition members, most of whom had agreed to support the revised version of S. 495. As hospitals prepared to lobby against the new draft legislation, the last dissenting member of the coalition, the Massachusetts Medical Society, agreed to support the bill. The lack of hospital support took its toll nonetheless; the bill lost momentum on the Senate floor despite extensive lobbying by business, physicians, Blue Cross, commercial insurers, and state government.

To secure hospital cooperation, the coalition agreed to ease socalled "productivity factors" for hospitals and to make implementation of the legislation contingent on securing Medicare's participation. The hospitals capitulated, and the Massachusetts legislature passed Chapter 372, perhaps the largest regulatory bill in the state's history, with little further debate. Apparently, legislators accepted the checks and balances inherent in such a diverse coalition of special interests as a proxy for thorough understanding of this complex legislation. Subsequently the governor secured agreement for Medicare participation from Richard Schweiker, the Health and Human Services secretary at that time.

Elements of the Legislation

It is not surprising that the basic financing mechanism of Blue Cross Hospital Contract HA–29 (the MAC) was adopted as the core of Chapter 372. The politically difficult task of getting hospitals to accept a new payment strategy had already been achieved with HA–29. Its complicated provisions were also being integrated into hospital operations. Extended to all payers, HA–29's incentives for efficiency and utilization control were strengthened. Finally, several negotiators of the Blue Cross Hospital Contract were members.

Arguably, the most contentious element of Chapter 372 is what became known as the "productivity factor," a 7.5 percent reduction in the allowable rate of annual inflation phased in over the first six years of the legislation. Hospital expenditures (about $3.6 billion) calculated from the base year of 1981 and compounded over the six year phase-in accounted for several hundred million dollars in cost avoidance. The business representatives insisted on the reduction for inflation, with the rationale that it would bring hospital costs closer to the national average.

Under Chapter 372, each hospital's budget is determined annually, based on its prior year's approved budget rather than on actual expenses. Moving from hospitals' audited expenses (including annualizations) in the base year (1981), adjustments are made for inflation plus 2–4 percent for volume and case-mix changes, new services, approved capital projects, and any other costs judged by an exceptions-review process to be beyond the hospital's control. The productivity factor is then subtracted from the aggregate index to determine a final allowance for annual increases.

Incentives to reduce volume and to shift procedures from inpatient to outpatient are based on marginal cost allowances. Hospitals are rewarded if they reduce admissions, lengths of stay, and ancillary services. They are penalized, with marginal costs fixed below actual incremental costs, for increases in inpatient admissions and in intensity of ancillary services. Another objective of the law is to reduce regulatory duplication and to implement a single audit process. Paperwork has been cut back, but negotiations concerning the scope and responsibility for the audit continue. Finally, hospitals are required to permit private payers to perform utilization review on care rendered to their beneficiaries.

Blue Cross plays a central role in the administration of Chapter 372. Its right to contract with hospitals is retained, and successor contracts to the original HA–29 are automatically substituted as Blue Cross's operative financing mechanism, although these contracts must be approved by the Rate Setting Commission.

A special commission established under Chapter 372 studied elements of the cost differential between Blue Cross and other private insurers. The panel defined and quantified components of the differential, such as Blue Cross's rapid claims payment, administrative efficiencies, and subsidies of nongroup coverage (for example, the over-65 Medex program). The allowable discount was reduced from 10.4 percent to 9 percent for fiscal years 1983–1984, after which the differential was determined based on economically justified criteria developed by the study commission. At that time, any payer complying with these criteria may apply to the commission for equal discounts.

Policy Issues

For public-policy purposes, it is interesting to compare provisions of Chapter 372 with the payment system of Medicare Diagnosis Related

Groups (DRGs), particularly because these two systems are viewed as different policy approaches to prospective payment.[2]

All-Payer versus One-Payer System. One major difference between the two prospective payment systems is that Chapter 372 is an all-payer system, while the Medicare DRG-based payment system applies to only one payer, Medicare, in most states. Under the Medicare system, hospitals may be able to recover losses from unprofitable DRGs by increasing prices to privately insured patients and others paying charges. Under the all-payer system in Chapter 372, differentials between levels of payment by public and private payers were frozen at 1981 levels, preventing further increases in cross-subsidization (cost shifting).

Calculating Costs of Treatment. A further important distinction between the two systems is the basis of payment in each. Chapter 372 limits total hospital budgets prospectively whereas the Medicare DRG system establishes prices on a per case basis for each diagnosis related group. The formulas used to calculate a hospital's budget under Chapter 372, though complex, do not require that the regulatory mechanism establish schedules of rates or become involved in issues such as how to update rates based on technological innovation. The formulas also create incentives for hospitals to control outpatient costs, inpatient admissions, ancillary use, and length of stay. In contrast, the Medicare DRG system must establish and update rates of payment for each of the 468 diagnosis-related groups. It must rely on extensive utilization review rather than on inherent financial incentives to control hospital admissions.

The differences between these prospective payment systems present an intriguing natural experiment. Comparison of the ability of each to control health care costs for all payers over time will indicate the appropriate direction for future health policy.

Chapter 372 has not solved the problem of health care costs in Massachusetts. In fact, one group's solution may be another's problem, as suggested by increases in both patient volume and level of medical needs reported by outpatient primary-care centers, visiting nursing groups, home health agencies, and nursing homes since the law took effect.

As a regulatory system, some aspects of Chapter 372 are arbitrary and unfair. For instance, because each hospital's budget is determined by actual 1981 base-year costs, those institutions that ran "fat," or inefficiently, in that base year are rewarded, and hospitals that controlled costs more effectively in the base year are penalized. The revenue streams of hospitals also vary according to patient mix, although relief was incorporated for hospitals like Boston City, which provide large amounts of care to patients who are uninsured.

Corrective legislation was passed in 1983 to help hospitals inappropriately penalized by the calculations based on the 1981 base year and also to address unintended technical errors in the bill. This legislation was developed by the Massachusetts Hospital Association and negotiated through the initial coalition, which still meets regularly to monitor implementation. At least one hospital has already filed special exemption legislation, contending that it could not survive under the law, but its bill was narrowly defeated.

The biggest loophole in the prospective formula is probably the automatic allotment of operating, interest, and depreciation costs that a hospital incurs from capital projects approved by the Determination of Need (DON) process. With $200–300 million in incremental costs linked to the billion dollars of applications pending when Chapter 372 was enacted, it is not surprising that payers immediately began an intense effort to slow approval of proposed DONs.

Summary

Chapter 372 was designed to slow the rate of increase of hospital expenditures, to prevent further cost shifting onto certain payers and to provide hospital managers with more rational incentives to improve efficiency. Members of the coalition believed that increased cost shifting would eventually drive the commercial insurers from the marketplace, and even Blue Cross agreed this scenario was unacceptable.

The all-payer legislation is the product of political compromise, shaped by a small group with vital and conflicting interests. Little meaningful financial analysis was available to evaluate alternatives or to project the effect of key provisions. At one point in the talks, a coalition member called the conclusions one could reach using numbers only "as soft as grapes." The final negotiations were conducted in private, with major constituencies including labor and the elderly, unrepresented.

Unfortunately, reliable data to evaluate the effect of Chapter 372's first year on hospital cost increases are scarce. Several studies of costs, services, and payer groups are underway, but results are not yet available. Chapter 372 appears to be functioning effectively as a short-term solution, slowing the rate of increase in hospital expenditures in Massachusetts. Its critics suggest, however, that it does little to encourage alternative delivery and financing systems that may offer better prospects for assuring cost-effective use of health care resources.

The waivers from the federal government, needed to allow Medicare to be included in the Massachusetts hospital payment system, expired on October 1, 1985. The federal government has tightened the conditions under which waivers will be granted, in part because it wants to ensure that it pays no more for Medicare under a state hospital payment system than it would pay under its DRG system. The hospitals would not accept the conditions under which a waiver would be granted. Hence, they pressured the state not to seek a waiver to include Medicare in the global budgeting system.

Because of this decision, the Health Care Coalition drafted legislation that would allow Medicare to begin payment under the federal DRG system starting October 1, 1985, while retaining the principles of Chapter 372 for other payers. For Medicaid and the private sector, liability will still be calculated based on a global budget defined under terms of the Blue Cross contract.

Private payers are concerned that when Medicare no longer pays its share hospitals will shift their costs to them. To address this concern, the proposed legislation puts a limit on charge increases to non-Medicare patients. The legislation also changes the method of payment for uncompensated care. Previously, under Chapter 372 each hospital had raised its charges to its privately insured patients and to Medicare and Medicaid to cover the costs of uncompensated care. The increases range from 2 percent to 114 percent at different hospitals. The proposed system would create a uniform statewide increase in charges (about 9.5 percent), and the additional money would be redistributed based on the actual cost of uncompensated care in each hospital. In effect, private payers whose patients are cared for in hospitals that provide much of the care for the indigent will bear less of the burden than they do now because it will be shared more equitably among private payers throughout the state.

The legislation passed in the fall of 1985.

Notes

1. "The Massachusetts Agenda—A Competitive Assessment of our Economy" (Boston: The Massachusetts Business Roundtable, 1983).

2. For Medicare participation in the Chapter 372 all-payer system, the Commonwealth receives a federal waiver from the Medicare DRG system.

4

The Unfinished Agenda for Medicaid Reform

Rosemary Gibson Kern

Introduction

This chapter examines the lessons learned from states' efforts to change the way Medicaid—the federal-state program that finances acute and long-term care for low-income persons—brings beneficiaries into contact with the health care system and pays the providers of care. The reforms enacted offer states the opportunity to provide better health care to Medicaid beneficiaries and, at the same time, to use health care resources more cost effectively.

These reforms have two principal thrusts. First, the states are changing patients' manner of access to health care services. For example, states are contracting with health maintenance organizations (HMOs), neighborhood health centers, hospitals, physician group practices, and individual physicians. These providers are serving as a patient's point of access to the health care system and as the patient's coordinator of care. Second, states are developing alternative, cost-effective arrangements for paying doctors, hospitals, and other health service providers. To do this, some states are modifying the traditional fee-for-service payment system; others are paying providers capitation or fixed payments.

Patients, providers, and the states are realizing benefits from changing the way Medicaid is administered. First, states are offering patients the opportunity to select a physician who serves as a patient's point of access to the health care system. The physician or case manager refers patients to other providers for care that is needed. Offering patients a regular source of care remedies the problem of many Medicaid patients of receiving health care services from several different providers, with no one provider aware of the patient's medical history and of all the care a patient may be currently receiving. A case manager also helps Medicaid patients find a physician to serve them.

51

Second, a complete record of a patient's care is available if the patient has a regular source of care. The states are thus more easily able to gather information on trends in the use of services, particularly the underuse of health care services, and on concerns related to the quality of care. Profiles of the care that patients receive offer states and providers a means of assessing the quality and quantity of patient care, in ways that were not possible under the fee-for-service system.

Third, states can offer providers some opportunity to increase their Medicaid reimbursement under capitation payments or modified fee-for-service. In some states, the low rate of Medicaid reimbursement under the fee-for-service system has discouraged physicians from participating in Medicaid. With limited participation of physicians, patient access to care can be hindered. Through the case management programs that encourage providers to render care cost effectively, the states are able to pay physicians a rate more comparable to the rate that private insurers pay on behalf of their beneficiaries.

These fundamental changes are in contrast to the short-term program changes, such as "freezes" on physicians' fees and reductions in eligibility and benefits that states have resorted to in times of budget crises. Short-term measures only temporarily relieve budget crises and postpone needed, long-term reform. The flexibility recently accorded to the states to operate their programs differently has allowed states to make fundamental changes in the provision of health care that allow for better use of health care resources.

Other reform efforts need to be made in the Medicaid program, however. Beneficiaries in different state Medicaid programs are offered widely varying benefits. In Tennessee, for example, Medicaid covers a maximum of fourteen hospital days per year whereas Medicaid in Ohio covers sixty hospital days per episode of illness. Taxpayers in different states are treated differently also. Those states with lower per capita incomes and lower tax bases that want to offer benefits comparable to those offered in a higher-income state must place a greater tax burden on their residents, as compared to the burden imposed on residents in wealthier states.

Given that states are being accorded a greater degree of flexibility to determine Medicaid eligibility, benefits, and methods of reimbursing providers, continued devolution of Medicaid policy making to the states offers many benefits but could also heighten the inequities among states' programs. Hence, ongoing reform is necessary to redress inequities resulting from the varying capabilities of the states to finance care for the poor. This chapter also outlines the agenda for continuing reform of the Medicaid program to correct for these inequities among the states.

Impetus for Reform

Medicaid Watershed in 1981. The current reshaping of Medicaid began with the federal Medicaid policy changes in the Omnibus Budget Reconciliation Act (OBRA) of 1981, which incorporated the most significant changes in the program since its inception in 1965. These changes in 1981 were made in the midst of an economic recession that put some states under enormous fiscal pressure that was compounded by federal Medicaid budget cuts. Congress used three tools in OBRA to legislate change: budget policy, reimbursement policy, and waiver authority. Each of the changes forced states to think differently about their programs.

Budget changes. The federal government's share of Medicaid expenditures ranges from 50 to 78 percent of states' Medicaid budgets, depending on the state's per capita income. Budget changes in the Omnibus Budget Reconciliation Act of 1981 decreased federal financing efforts in Medicaid. The act cut the growth in federal expenditures by $0.5 billion in 1982. Through 1984, OBRA cuts totaled $2.0 billion. These decreases were the result of a cut in federal Medicaid dollars to the states—3 percent in 1982, 4 percent in 1983, and 4½ percent in 1984. These reductions were offset in states that had unemployment rates greater than 150 percent of the national average, a qualified hospital cost-review program, or demonstrated recoveries from fraud and abuse control.

Lower-income states, which receive higher federal matching rates, were more deeply affected by the flat percentage decrease in the federal contribution. They would have had to pay a greater percentage of their current share to make up for the loss in federal dollars. Wealthier states with lower federal matching rates had a proportionately lower cut.

Congress also gave the states greater flexibility to reduce Medicaid spending by changing Medicaid benefits and limiting eligibility. OBRA provisions allowed states to offer different benefits to different categories of eligibles in their programs for the medically needy. Also, OBRA included provisions to restrict eligibility for Aid to Families with Dependent Children (AFDC), which automatically restricts Medicaid eligibility. For example, the statute placed a cap on the gross income a family could have and still be eligible. The cap was set at 150 percent of a state's need standard. Six states raised their need standards to neutralize some of the effect of the income cap on eligibility.

Hospital reimbursement changes. Congress also made Medicaid program changes in OBRA, allowing states to change the way they pay

53

physicians and administer their programs and limiting the recipients' choice of provider. The program changes also allow the states to develop their own ways of paying hospitals. Previously, the states had to pay hospitals according to Medicare's open-ended, cost-based reimbursement system. This requirement precluded states from negotiating contracts with hospitals that agreed to provide care at predetermined rates.

States have responded in a variety of ways. California is negotiating contracts with hospitals that are paid on a per diem basis. Other states, including Pennsylvania, Michigan, and Ohio, have implemented a variation of Medicare's diagnosis-related group (DRG) system.

Waiver authority. In addition to using budget policy as a tool for policy making, Congress offered states the opportunity to administer their programs differently by allowing the Department of Health and Human Services (HHS) to waive federal Medicaid regulations. Through waivers, states have been able to pay physicians a set fee or capitation payment rather than a fee-for-service payment. They can also establish case management programs that link patients with a solo or group practice physician or with an HMO. States can also contract with organizations that help to administer the Medicaid program and that bear some financial risk in doing so.

The traditional purpose of the waiver process has been to allow HHS to conduct demonstrations on alternative delivery and financing schemes. They offer the federal government a way to strike a balance between making incentives-based reform mandatory, which would force market changes that may be untimely and inappropriate in certain areas, and leaving the program as is. At issue is at what point waivers and demonstrations offer sufficient testing of key features to give Congress information on whether they should legislate statutory changes. Without eventual legislative changes, states will be subject to the vagaries of waiver-renewal processes if they want to continue their Medicaid reform efforts.

Reshaping Medicaid: Lessons Learned

A number of lessons are being learned as states and local entities experiment with some form of case management, capitation payment, and modified fee-for-service arrangements. Although case management and capitation are not new to health care delivery and financing, they are relatively new to the Medicaid program. In future years, the states will be fine-tuning these concepts as they are implemented.

Thus far, some experiments have failed, such as Kentucky's

Citicare program and California's Monterey County health initiative.[1] Others, such as Missouri's managed-care program and California's Santa Barbara health initiative, are making headway in determining the key elements of success in changing the way providers, consumers, and even the program administrators work with Medicaid.[2] Examples of two different approaches in Massachusetts—the Commonwealth Health Care Corporation and the state's case management program—are examined by Susan Windham in this volume.

Analysis of the states' experiments has proceeded through several stages. Initially, policy research focused primarily on states' fiscal problems aggravated by the open-ended, fee-for-service reimbursement system. Research then began to describe the general approach states have been taking to change the way health services are provided and financed. A few studies have systematically examined the reasons for success or failure of earlier experiments—the Safeco United Healthcare program in the state of Washington and Project Health, a program for the medically needy in Oregon.[3] Only initial steps have been made in analyzing some of the reasons for success or failure in some of the recent Medicaid demonstrations. Some collected wisdom can be gleaned, though, from preliminary research on the implementation of the states' experiments.[4]

A Voluntary or Mandatory Program? One of the decisions a state has to make in establishing a case management program is whether beneficiaries will have a choice about participating. Budgetary pressure to save program dollars encourages a policy of mandatory enrollment. Mandatory enrollment would, however, still allow patients to choose their primary care providers or case managers.

Programs with mandatory enrollment offer states the advantage of administering one Medicaid program rather than two programs (a traditional and an experimental one). If a mandatory program has to be abandoned, though, the transition back to the traditional Medicaid program could cause significant disruption. The transition from an experimental project to a state-run program in Monterey County, whose demonstration has been discontinued because of substantial operating deficits, will indicate the extent of adjustments that may need to be made in other jurisdictions.

Consumer-oriented groups generally encourage a system of voluntary enrollment to allow beneficiaries free choice of providers. Under voluntary enrollment, the patient can choose to be "locked-in" to a selected provider or to an HMO. The advantage of voluntary enrollment for the states is that they have the flexibility to implement the program step by step. New Jersey's Medicaid experiment and the

Massachusetts case management program are examples of a voluntary program.

Programs operating on a voluntary basis necessarily limit their pool of beneficiaries. From the Safeco experience, program administrators have learned that case managers, who have only a few patients enrolled in the experimental programs, are insulated from the incentive effects of a payment system that encourages physician case managers to use resources wisely. In contrast, physician case managers with a large number of Medicaid beneficiaries enrolled in a capitation payment system have much greater incentive to use resources wisely; the physician can reap some benefit from providing cost-effective care and could be at some minimal risk for not doing so. Hence, changing only the reimbursement system does not ensure that case managers will allocate resources cost effectively. In order to change their practice patterns, physicians need enough enrollees to make a difference financially.

Setting Capitation Rates. States that choose to pay physician case managers, HMOs, or neighborhood health centers on a capitation basis rather than under a modified fee-for-service system find that setting capitation rates is one of the more difficult tasks in establishing a state experiment. A number of lessons have been learned about calculating rates to reflect the cost of providing care to beneficiaries. Some researchers have found that criteria used to set capitation rates—age, sex, and welfare category—may be insufficient predictors of future use of health care services. Past utilization rates have been suggested as much more precise predictors of future use.

Yet other research shows that prior utilization trends may not necessarily be good estimates of future use. Overestimates result if prior use includes inefficiency. If, for example, there was a high rate of emergency room use for nonemergency care, the fee-for-service base would reflect this inefficient use of resources; or, if patients were "doctor shopping" and taking multiple prescriptions when they were not in need of such treatment, then the base from which the capitation rates were calculated would include inappropriate expenditures.

Underestimates of future use result if patients using the fee-for-service system had difficulty gaining access to care and did not receive continuity of care. Prenatal care presents an example of how utilization in the fee-for-service system can underestimate future use of health services in a case management, capitated system. For case managers to provide proper prenatal care, they would likely be providing more care to some patients than the patients would have sought or received under fee-for-service. Rates based on underuse do not reflect the cost of providing continuity of prenatal care. Because of this problem, some programs have excluded prenatal care and delivery from capitation rates. Given the imprecision in rate setting, researchers need to focus on how states are setting rates for the Medicaid population and how providers render care within those rates.

Assuring Quality Care. Under a case management system that incorporates capitation payments, there is a need for quality assurance. Some observers point to the built-in incentives to providers to underserve patients in a capitation system. These incentives are in contrast to the incentives in a fee-for-service system where quality of care could be jeopardized by providing too much care.

Grievance procedures can generate some indication of whether physicians are underproviding care. Because grievance procedures rely on beneficiaries' submitting grievances, they offer little systematic appraisal of quality. Such an appraisal requires researchers to compare provider practice patterns under the fee-for-service system and under an innovative system.

Because such information on utilization and quality has not generally been collected under the fee-for-service payment system, it is difficult to make "before and after" comparisons of quality. Comparisons can be made, though, with trends in the use of health care services in ongoing fee-for-service programs.

Case management allows the states to enter a new era in monitoring the quality of patient care. Some states are beginning to document, by patient and case manager, trends in physician visits, hospital use, referrals to specialists, and emergency-room use. Some changes in the kinds of care provided are anticipated, such as a decline in the number of referrals and in the use of emergency rooms in nonemergency situations. The quality-related issue is whether such changes reflect decreased use of necessary or unnecessary care. Some states have set up peer review committees to assess, often on a random basis, the quality of patient care.

There is often a lag time before states can accumulate enough experience under the programs to perform utilization review and quality assurance. States need to collect sufficient information and develop a system to produce reports on patient care. Some of the experiments, however, have had difficulty developing such reports.

Program Management. Encouraging the judicious use of health care services is one of the important features of state experiments. The capitation payment systems offer some means of encouraging providers to allocate resources cost effectively. Also, the case management structure itself helps patients and providers use resources wisely. For the capitation and case management functions to work, however, and in the absence of a capitation payment system, several checks in the systems need to be established.

First, referral care needs to be closely monitored. Some patients may refer themselves to specialty care or emergency room care without authorization from the case manager. Without controls, care may be provided without the case manager's knowledge. Some programs, like the Santa Barbara initiative, have set up strict referral authorization procedures which, while administratively burdensome, try to prevent unauthorized referral care.

Other programs, like the Monterey County, California, demonstration and Safeco's, realized only in hindsight the importance of strict oversight of the use of referral services. In the initial stages there appeared to be a lag in the use of services and the reporting of claims, causing liabilities to be understated. As use of services increased, program managers realized that they needed to tighten controls. In the Safeco experiment, protocols for length of stay and outpatient surgery were established. Yet the experiment was terminated shortly after these changes were implemented because of mounting deficits.

Good program management requires that case managers receive reports on the claims paid for care rendered to their patients by referral providers. This information enables the provider to know that the patient followed the recommended treatment. Good program management also requires that providers receive information on their overall financial status, especially under a capitation payment system, which puts them at some financial risk.

A related management issue is whether case managers should choose their own referral specialists. Some observers believe that a management team should choose high- and low-cost referral physicians and hospitals to help defray the information and search costs for case managers. Other program administrators would rather see each primary care physician choose his or her own referral physicians.

Program administrators also need to weigh the advantages and disadvantages of attaining the support of local hospitals by allowing all of them to participate. In both Santa Barbara and Monterey, all of the hospitals signed contracts with the authorities administering the two programs. Although such an arrangement allows for amicable relations in the community, it could preclude the possibility of obtaining a lower rate of reimbursement through selective contracting. In California the state contracts selectively with hospitals throughout the state, whereas the Santa Barbara program contracts with all hospitals in the county. The administrators of the Santa Barbara initiative believe that the rates they pay hospitals are comparable to rates they could have negotiated under the selective-contracting program. Hence, they believe they have achieved two objectives—better access to care and acceptable hospital rates.

Managing High-Risk Patients. Program administrators are learning the possibilities as well as the limits of managing the care of high-risk patients. Some programs have excluded Supplemental Security Income (SSI) beneficiaries from participating because they tend to be high-risk patients. In programs enrolling only AFDC eligibles, some administrators have had to allow physicians to drop particularly sick and high-cost patients from their practices. In the Santa Barbara County experiment, all Medicaid beneficiaries are included in the experiment, but program managers have recognized the difficulty of controlling the use of services for very sick, disabled, or handicapped persons. Individual physicians are therefore not at financial risk for patients designated as high risks. Also, for some patients, the authority administering the demonstration receives 100 percent of charges from the state rather than the usual 95 percent.

Cost Savings. The potential for immediate cost savings from case management programs should not be overblown. Researchers need to assess the short- and long-term outlook for program savings as well as the quantifiable and nonquantifiable benefits from the programs. It would be a mistake to judge the viability and desirability of these programs solely on whether they achieve immediate cost savings. Researchers also need to assess the extent to which the programs can offer access to the health care system to those who would otherwise not have such access. Moreover, if providers can render care more effectively to patients under a case management program, and if incentives encourage more providers to participate in Medicaid, then the program may provide better care and increased access that cannot easily be translated into cost savings.

Although the Medicaid experiments' own features and the manner of their implementation are important determinants of the shape and the success of each program, the activity in a geographical area may be a major determinant of the degree of influence the incentives can have on providers and, hence, on the potential cost savings. The fiscal pressure from other payers—Medicare, HMOs, preferred-provider organizations, and other alternative health plans—can have a tremendous effect on the receptivity of providers toward participation, ease of implementation, and ultimately, cost savings in the Medicaid program. Also, the number of physicians and hospital beds in

59

the market area can affect the degree to which cost savings can be realized in Medicaid. Thus, the potential for cost savings can vary, depending on the environment in which health care providers are working.

Agenda for Continued Research

The test of the experiments in case-management programs is whether they can achieve three goals: (1) quality care for Medicaid patients; (2) sufficient income for providers to assure their participation in programs serving persons to whom the federal and state governments have made commitments; and (3) control of the rate of increase in the cost of health care.

To determine whether the experiments meet these goals, research needs to focus on several areas of inquiry. One crucial area for research is the changing patterns of utilization under the new incentives. For example:

• Has emergency room use for nonemergency care decreased significantly?

• Given that financial incentives may not be sufficient to change provider behavior, are changes in practice patterns less marked among physicians with fewer enrollees because of decreased visibility of the program and its incentives?

• Are lower-cost forms of care, such as skilled nursing facility services and home care becoming more available as a substitute for higher-cost hospital care?

• To what extent are practice patterns changing for case managers who share risk with other providers?

• What information do case managers receive on the care they have rendered and referred? Is the information sufficient to allow physicians to keep track of all of their patients' care?

Closely related to the changes in patterns of utilization is how physicians manage patient care. Each physician probably defines and implements the case management function differently. Evaluators need to ask:

• How do different providers—physicians, hospitals, neighborhood health centers, and HMOs—define their case management role?

• Is case management being implemented with the rigor to make it work? For example, are hospital emergency room personnel notifying case managers when patients come for nonemergency care? Are patients seeking care from other providers without authorization from their case managers?

- Have program administrators found it necessary or desirable to develop protocols to serve as guides for physicians in their decisions to refer patients to other providers or for hospital inpatient care?
- Have case managers had success in managing high-risk patients? Is prenatal care excluded from capitation rates because of the potential for exposure to undue risk?
- To what extent and for what reasons are case managers changing the specialists to whom they are referring their patients?
- Is prior authorization required for physicians to perform certain services? What kind of utilization review system is in place? How have these mechanisms worked?

Research needs to be undertaken on the effect of the programs on the quality of care that is provided. Questions to be asked include:

- How has the substitution of lower-cost for higher-cost care changed the quality of care rendered to Medicaid patients?
- What criteria have been established to prompt review of cases by the program's medical director?
- For what kinds of cases or types of case managers is there concern about the quality of care rendered?
- How reliable is the grievance procedure in calling attention to aberrant practice patterns?
- Are there any diagnoses that are being especially well managed or poorly managed under case management?

The Medicaid experiments are being conducted in a rapidly changing health care environment that can have a catalytic effect on their implementation. Researchers need to determine:

- whether providers have had experience with case management, capitation, or modified fee-for-service arrangements prior to the experiment;
- what new preferred provider organization (PPO) or HMO activity has been taking place in the local geographic area;
- whether there is an "oversupply" of physicians in the community. Has this spurred physicians to participate in Medicaid?
- whether the suppression of fees under the Medicaid program has discouraged physicians. Does the possibility of higher reimbursement under the experiments attract more physicians to participate in Medicaid?

Ongoing research will help to explain why certain programs succeed and others fail and will be especially useful to programs that are being developed. In October 1984, the Robert Wood Johnson Foundation awarded grants totaling $13 million to establish case management programs for Medicaid beneficiaries and other low-income persons. Also, New York is establishing managed-care programs for Medicaid beneficiaries in several areas of the state. It is likely that case management, modified fee-for-service arrangements, and capitation payments will be features incorporated in many, if not most Medicaid programs in the years to come.

Other Items on the Medicaid Reform Agenda

Inequities among Beneficiaries and Taxpayers. In addition to the structural changes in the way care is provided and financed under Medicaid, other items remain on the Medicaid reform agenda. The variations in eligibility criteria and covered benefits among the states' programs have been well documented.[5] Because of eligibility restrictions, almost half of the persons below poverty income levels are not eligible for Medicaid. Moreover, for those who are eligible the benefits in lower-income states are often more limited in scope than the benefits in higher-income states.

Some providers bear significant costs in treating the non-Medicaid-eligible poor and in rendering services to Medicaid beneficiaries that are not covered under the program. As the burden of the uninsured is being recognized in some states, and as many states' financial situations have improved, some states have expanded the scope of their Medicaid programs. In 1983 and 1984 twenty-four states expanded Medicaid eligibility, and fourteen states added or extended benefits. Other states have undertaken more comprehensive efforts by establishing programs to finance care for the medically indigent. On the federal level, in the 1984 Deficit Reduction Act, Medicaid coverage was extended to include women pregnant for the first time and children under age five.

Of particular interest are the efforts of Florida and South Carolina to finance uncompensated care. Their programs combine private- and public-sector funding as a means of financing both Medicaid and care rendered to poor persons not eligible for Medicaid. Florida established a program for the medically needy in 1984 and expanded eligibility to include low-income children in two-parent families, married pregnant women, and families with unemployed primary-wage earners. Unlike other state programs that have been expanded, Florida's program for the medically needy is financed largely by a 1 percent tax on all Florida hospitals' revenues.

South Carolina has enacted legislation that includes a provision for establishing a program for the care of the medically indigent financed by the counties and hospitals. This program is for persons not eligible for Medicaid but who are too poor to pay for their care. Also, the state will expand the eligibility and benefits in the Medicaid program by providing coverage for families with an unemployed parent who meet the Medicaid income and asset tests, and eliminating the twelve-day limit on inpatient hospital stays.

These measures, although useful, do not address the inequities underlying the program. Several studies have documented how adjustments in the formula used to determine the federal share of a state's program, which actually favors high-income rather than low-income states, can be adjusted to redress some of the inequities. With these adjustments, other states may be encouraged to expand the scope of their Medicaid programs.

Changing the Federal Matching Formula. Because the federal matching formula accounts for states' per capita income, one would think that lower-income states would receive more federal dollars per beneficiary than higher-income states. Instead, wealthier states that can afford richer benefits receive more federal dollars per Medicaid beneficiary because their lower matching rate is applied to a larger base of benefits and a larger scope of eligibility. In contrast, some lower-income states have a larger federal match applied to a smaller benefit package and receive fewer federal dollars per beneficiary.

As an example, Mississippi, which has a relatively low per capita income, had a 77-percent federal matching rate that is applied to a lean benefits package and received an average of $529 per beneficiary in fiscal year 1980. A wealthier state like Connecticut, which had a 50-percent federal matching rate received $805 per beneficiary in 1980. As a state with a lower per capita income and lower tax base, Mississippi chooses not to impose on its residents the higher tax rates that would be necessary to offer benefits comparable to those offered in higher-income states. Hence, substantial inequity among the state programs occurs even with federal matching.

Alternatives to the current method of calculating the federal match would resolve some of the inequity among beneficiaries and taxpayers. Currently, the formula uses per capita income as an indicator of the size of the poor population and of the states' ability to pay for the Medicaid program. Research findings show that better indicators of a state's ability to pay exist. For example, although both Nevada and the District of Columbia have the same per capita income and therefore the same federal match, the district has twice the number of people with incomes below poverty levels. Hence, including the number of persons with incomes below poverty in the formula would address some of the current inequity.

63

The state's revenue base or taxing capacity is another factor that could be better accounted for in the effort to eliminate some of the inequity among taxpayers. As an example, while Connecticut and the District of Columbia spend approximately the same per Medicaid eligible, the District's tax effort is about 135 percent greater than that of Connecticut.[6] The reason is that Connecticut's revenue base, relative to the number of people in poverty, is more than two times greater than the District's. If the Medicaid formula accounted for the state's varying tax capacities, lower-income state. vould have to make less sacrifice to offer benefits that are comparable to those offered in higher-income states.

Capping Medicaid Expenditures. Several proposals to freeze federal Medicaid expenditures or to cut federal Medicaid expenditures by a flat percentage have been discussed by policy makers as short-term budget control measures. These proposals, like the 1981 OBRA limits on the federal contribution to Medicaid, would exacerbate the inequity that already exists in the program.

A freeze or a cap would require states to cover 100 percent of the cost of any real increase in Medicaid expenditures. Lower-income states would have less incentive to expand Medicaid coverage. Expanding the scope of their Medicaid programs would require them to pay a proportionally larger increase than higher-income states. For Mississippi, which pays 23 percent of Medicaid expenditures, the effective cost of paying for any real increase in expenditures would increase from 23 percent to 100 percent, a fourfold increase. A higher-income state with a 50 percent contribution would have the effective cost of any real increase in spending jump from 50 percent to 100 percent, a twofold increase.

Thus, by changing the factors in the Medicaid formula and by rejecting a policy that caps federal expenditures, the federal government can encourage poorer states to offer more generous programs. They would have incentive to raise their low maximum-income eligibility standards, which currently preclude Medicaid eligibility for many persons with incomes below the poverty line. Also, a sliding scale of eligibility for Medicaid and welfare could be implemented for persons who are in transition from nonworking poor to working poor. This sliding scale for eligibility would recognize that although a person is employed, he is not often immediately wealthy enough to afford health insurance. These changes would not eliminate all the gaps in the system, but they could raise the minimum benefits and expand eligibility.

To finance these and other additional commitments to the Medicaid program, policy makers need to reconsider existing commitments to allocate resources for people who are most in need. In particular, commitments made to middle- and upper-income persons eligible for Medicare need to be scrutinized because age is not necessarily a relevant factor in determining need. Also, policy makers need to reconsider the tax benefit accorded to persons whose employer-paid health insurance is tax-free income to the employee. The need to reexamine this tax expenditure is particularly compelling since it benefits primarily middle- and upper-income persons.

Conclusion

In the long term, states and counties will continue to experiment with case management and with variations of capitation and fee-for-service payments to providers. Researchers need to assess the effect of these experiments on the quality of patient care. Also, researchers need to document the reasons for the success or failure of the programs. Long-term as well as short-term outlooks are needed for an accurate appraisal of the potential for managed-care programs to provide better care more cost effectively. "Quick fixes" that force providers, administrators, and consumers to adjust too rapidly are likely to generate, at least in the short term, inefficient responses and problems in quality.

Yet Medicaid reformers should not rest, content with trying to allocate existing resources more cost effectively. Other items on the Medicaid reform agenda that would redress inequities among taxpayers and, especially among beneficiaries, need to be brought to the fore of the policy debate. Changing the formula for federal matching funds for Medicaid to account for a state's poverty population and a state's taxing capacity could encourage states with lower per capita incomes to offer benefits to uninsured persons. Capping federal Medicaid expenditures would exacerbate the current inequities. These and other changes in the scope of the Medicaid program could be financed from revenues currently allocated to persons who are less in need of public support. These changes would allow for more persons who are poor to be included in a restructured Medicaid program that offers easier access and continuity of care.

Notes

1. See Deborah Freund, *Medicaid Reform: Four Case Studies in Case Management* (Washington, D.C.: American Enterprise Institute, 1984), pp. 37–56, for a discussion of the Kentucky Citicare program. See also, Sean Sullivan, *The*

Monterey County Health Initiative (Washington, D.C.: American Enterprise Institute, June 1984), unpublished report, for a discussion of the Monterey County program.

2. See Maren Anderson, *The Missouri Managed Health Care Program* (Washington, D.C.: Lewin and Associates, June 1984) for an analysis of Missouri's program. See also, Rosemary Gibson Kern, *The Santa Barbara Health Initiative* (Washington, D.C.: American Enterprise Institute, June 1984), unpublished report, for an examination of Santa Barbara's experience in a managed care program.

3. In 1978 the SAFECO life insurance company organized United Healthcare as a primary-care network for privately insured patients. See Stephen Moore, Diane Martin, and William Richardson, "Does the Primary Care Gatekeeper Control the Costs of Health Care?" *The New England Journal of Medicine* (December 1, 1983), pp. 1400–04, for an analysis of SAFECO's experiment. Project Health was a program started in 1973 to provide health care to medically indigent persons. See also, Jurgovan and Blair, Inc., *An Evaluation of Project Health Medically Needy Demonstration* (November 1981), unpublished report.

4. An evaluation of seven Medicaid case management demonstrations is being conducted by a consortium of researchers from the Research Triangle Institute, the University of North Carolina at Chapel Hill, the Medical College of Virginia, the American Enterprise Institute, and Lewin and Associates under contract with the Health Care Financing Administration.

5. Thomas Grannemann and Mark Pauly, *Controlling Medicaid Costs* (Washington, D.C.: American Enterprise Institute, 1983), pp. 21–28. See also, Karen Davis and Cathy Schoen, *Health and the War on Poverty* (Washington, D.C.: Brookings Institution, 1978), pp. 52–56.

6. General Accounting Office, *Changing Medicaid Formula Can Improve Distribution of Funds to States*, March 9, 1983, p.ii.

5

New Ways of Paying for Medicare and Medicaid: Summary of Conference Proceedings

Introduction

AEI's Center for Health Policy Research recently concluded a series of ten bimonthly conferences under a grant from the Pew Memorial Trust. These conferences, which were held from September 1982 to October 1984, focused on states' and counties' efforts to change the way health care is provided and financed under Medicaid. State officials were offered a forum in which they could discuss among themselves the steps being taken to change the structure of Medicaid financing and delivery. The conferences also enabled the center's staff to understand the dynamics of incentives-based reforms in health care.

This summary documents the proceedings of the last conference in the series, held on October 19, 1984. Several local demonstration projects testing new ways of paying for care under Medicare and Medicaid were the focus of discussion. The Medicaid demonstrations are testing the effectiveness of case management under capitation and variations on fee for service in seven sites. The Medicare demonstrations are testing the effect of Medicare beneficiaries' enrollment in health maintenance organizations (HMOs).

The purpose of the conference was to allow researchers evaluating federal Medicaid and Medicare demonstrations to discuss some of their preliminary findings. The conference also sought to address how interim findings can be useful to public policy makers, who must often make decisions without the benefit of final analyses and evaluations. In another session, not summarized here, the evaluators discussed the status of the Medicare HMO demonstrations and the Medicaid case management demonstrations.

Session 1: Common Implementation Issues

This session addressed two main issues:

- the nature of the competition taking place in the market areas where Medicare and Medicaid demonstrations are being implemented
- the way in which case management is being implemented, particularly in the Medicaid demonstrations

The Nature of the Competition. The demonstrations had their roots in the movement to institute incentives for providers and patients to use health resources wisely. Advocates of incentives-based reform hoped that both the private and the public sectors could achieve savings from a streamlined health care system while improving access to care for the populations served by these programs.

The first part of the session focused on the degree of competition actually taking place in the demonstration market areas. The following questions were addressed:

- Is competition or merely prepayment being tested in the demonstrations?
- Are providers competing for enrollees on the basis of price or benefits?
- Insofar as competition is taking place, how does it differ in the Medicare and Medicaid demonstration market areas?

Medicare. Evaluators of the Medicare HMO demonstrations observed that HMOs are competing in a variety of ways and that the demonstrations they are studying go well beyond merely testing the efficacy of prepayment. In Florida, for example, HMOs are competing with companies offering Medicare supplemental insurance. The HMOs are offering more attractive benefit packages than many of the insurers, with some HMOs even including lifetime hospital benefits to encourage beneficiaries to enroll. HMOs are also setting their premiums at a rate slightly lower than the premiums charged by insurance carriers. There thus appears to be competition on the basis of both price and benefits. One evaluator raised the point that competition for enrollees adds to the HMOs' operating costs, particularly for marketing.

Medicaid. In contrast, in the Medicaid demonstration areas, providers are typically not competing for patients on the basis of price or benefits. Unlike Medicare providers, Medicaid providers are not willing to augment the standard Medicaid package to encourage patients to enroll, in part, because they perceive Medicaid payments as generally insufficient to cover a larger benefit package.

Providers are also not competing with one another on the basis of price. In all but one of the demonstrations, the state or authority administering the demonstration pays capitation rates, based on the type of patient enrolled, that are the same for all providers. The exception to this rule is the Arizona Health Care Cost Containment System (AHCCCS) demonstration, where providers are submitting bids to the state to provide Medicaid services.

Although providers are generally not competing on the basis of benefits or price under Medicaid pilot projects, they are competing for patients to the extent that they do not want to lose their market share. An additional incentive for providers to participate is that some of the demonstrations, notably those in New Jersey and Santa Barbara, California, have distributed surpluses to some physicians after the first operating year. Yet even providers who want to participate are often reluctant to make a commitment to expand their current capacity to serve more Medicaid patients, given the uncertain future of the demonstrations.

Unlike the Medicare providers, who conduct their own advertising, many of the Medicaid demonstrations preclude direct marketing and advertising by providers. Where such marketing is allowed, it is closely overseen by the demonstration administrator. A program administrator of one Medicaid demonstration cited the need for the program to strike a balance between overregulating and underregulating providers.

Some discussants were doubtful whether competition could even be said to be operating in the demonstrations, given that a single buyer, namely Medicare or Medicaid, wields substantial market power. A truly competitive system requires numerous buyers and sellers.

The Nature of Case Management. In the second half of the session case management was discussed. Case management is a system in which a physician or a prepaid plan serves as a point of access to all health care services that an enrolled patient requires. The case manager is in charge of making all referrals and serves as an allocator of limited resources. Patients relinquish their choice of provider once they have chosen a case manager.

Some participants expressed concern that the combination of the case manager and resource allocator roles offers providers incentives to underrefer patients. One participant raised the related issue that the states have very little information on how physicians provide care as case managers or how case management affects the quality of care. A discussant responded that HMOs' experience with case management offers a good deal of information on both these questions. Yet some uncertainty was expressed concerning whether the reduced utilization in HMOs stems from a change in practice that relates directly to the benefits of case management or whether it is simply a consequence of pressure to constrain costs.

Some of the researchers indicated the states' need for information on physicians' patterns of use under case management and on how medical decisions are affected by payment incentives. One participant stressed that in evaluating a case management demonstration, researchers need to determine what features are workable and why a particular model was successful.

In response to these concerns several participants stressed that the drawbacks of case management need to be considered in the context of the disadvantages in patterns of care under a fee-for-service system. Fee-for-service payments, combined with unlimited choice of providers, create the unsatisfactory situation in which many patients receive episodic primary care in emergency rooms and lack the benefits of an ongoing relationship with a provider who offers a point of access to care.

One participant stressed the special case of maternity and prenatal care in case management systems. Concern was expressed that capitation systems have been based on the assumption that a substantial amount of unnecessary care is provided. Yet the Medicaid population generally underuses prenatal care. Hence, capitation rates that are set without regard to the underuse of certain services do not encourage providers to render the full scope of prenatal care when the payment does not reflect the greater services needed.

A representative of one of the demonstration projects noted that the program's managers changed the way the program paid providers for obstetrical care because similar concerns had been expressed by physicians. They decided to relieve physicians of any financial risk for providing prenatal and obstetrical care.

The representative also indicated ways in which the demonstrations can safeguard the quality of care. In one demonstration the medical director has the authority to override any physician's decision on referrals. Questions on denials of referrals come to the medical director's attention through the grievance process and through the information systems that track patterns of use. Some researchers pointed out, however, that other demonstrations are not as far along in developing their data systems to provide information on how resources are allocated and medical decisions are made under case management.

One of the evaluation tasks is to account for the surpluses physicians have received. Are they attributable to adverse selection, overgenerous payment rates, denial of needed referrals, or denial of unnecessary care?

A final point suggested the need for a long-range view of the competition that might be taking place in the market. It may be that providers who offer less attractive benefits or amenities or a perceived lower quality of care will have decreasing enrollments while those offering more satisfactory care will gradually gain new enrollees.

Session 2: The Role of Research in Policy Making

In the afternoon session the participants discussed the steps that need to be taken to translate the research findings from the demonstrations into policy to produce better Medicare and Medicaid programs. Much of the discussion centered on dissemination—how does the right information reach the right people? Many researchers, it was argued, circulate their findings among a small circle of academic colleagues, and the information often fails to reach policy makers.

It was further noted that sending legislators the kinds of information the program evaluators tend to generate—detailed 200–300 page reports—is of little use. While the audience for these lengthy reports is clearly limited, a number of participants mentioned the need for researchers to strike a balance between giving the policy makers a 300-page report and providing a simplistic, "comic book" version of their work. The consensus on how this balance should be obtained was to provide (along with or instead of the full report) an executive summary of the experimental program, which should highlight:

- the problem the program addresses
- a general description of the program
- why the program has or has not succeeded
- the implementation plan for those wishing to replicate the program

Participants agreed that the information the research community provides generally overemphasizes the second of these, description of the plan, and too often ignores the third and fourth. Researchers tend to explain in minute detail a program's complex payment system—but fail to give adequate attention to why the initiative succeeded and how it can be replicated. The evaluators need to ask the right questions.

Regarding replication, the participants expressed the concern that

71

many practitioners, such as those starting HMOs, begin their ventures without the benefit of research. The research community has information that would help entrepreneurs in the private and public sectors, both in showing why previous experiments worked and in describing the process by which they became operational. Researchers can rescue the replicators from many of the growing pains of the experimental program by recounting how the obstacles to implementation were overcome. This information can and should be disseminated early in the evaluation process, rather than withheld until the final report is ready—often three or more years later.

Disseminating Interim Findings. The need to disseminate research findings in a usable form for program implementers and policy makers prompted a discussion of what the role of preliminary judgments and interim findings ought to be. Some participants argued that by the time the demonstration runs its course and the final evaluation report is written and made available, the rest of the actors in our rapidly changing health care system have, for better or worse, already taken action. Thus interim findings must be made available if these experiments are to be relevant to projects in the early stages of development.

Other participants pointed to the dangers of basing policy decisions on interim findings, arguing that preliminary findings are often inaccurate and that researchers might lead the policy makers down the wrong path. The participants acknowledged that researchers are often too anxious to have an impact, that policy makers are often too anxious to take action, and that both these factors increase the potential pitfalls of early dissemination.

A number of participants agreed that the way researchers present the interim results is a crucial factor in ensuring that policy makers are aware of the limitations of the study or its findings and that they do not unknowingly overreact to preliminary or inconclusive results. They also agreed that current long-term evaluations may help policy makers make better policy decisions in the short term and also have an important effect on future decision making. One discussant suggested that in designing complicated, multiyear evaluations, research agendas should build in automatic points of dissemination, such as conferences, seminars, and briefings.

The Research Agenda. The discussion turned to the important role played by the Department of Health and Human Services (HHS) in forecasting what the future policy issues will be and in tailoring the research agenda to address those issues. An HHS official stated that the department has made a strong effort to establish an oversight system to determine what the evaluation agenda should be and that as a result the department's studies are better aimed at what the future decisions are expected to be rather than what individual researchers want to do.

Another participant urged that the research agenda not be determined solely by high-level HHS officials, whose view of what the future issues will be could be politically slanted in any administration. It was argued that the foundation and university communities need to fill in the gaps in the government's research agenda, although they cannot be expected to fund the elaborate demonstration-evaluation projects that the federal government finances.

Dissemination to the States. Participants in state Medicaid initiatives noted that getting the right information to state rather than federal officials is a different and perhaps more difficult task, given the states' variety of interests and smaller staffs. One state official asserted that no information would be more helpful than the experiences of other Medicaid demonstrations.

One participant argued that this sort of dissemination should be a natural outgrowth of the Reagan administration's New Federalism. If the federal government's goal is to loosen up regulations to allow for increased flexibility and experimentation, it ought to play a greater role in disseminating information on how the innovations are working.

Another participant asserted that the problem of reaching the states has been made out to be more difficult than it is and that researchers need only send reports to each of the fifty state Medicaid directors. From there, they will be duplicated and distributed.

Turning Waivers into Policy. The conference concluded with a discussion of when and how regulatory provisions should be changed rather than simply waived. When have demonstrations accumulated enough experience and information to indicate that a program ought to be changed? Will the Medicare and Medicaid programs be the same five years from now in spite of all the research that has been funded and conducted? Several participants pointed to the highly political nature of the policy process, in which demonstration results are but one of several factors influencing the decision makers. They concluded that the degree to which the waivers promote policy change is largely out of the hands of the researchers.

Others discussed the diverging perceptions of the waiver process. The federal government views waiver projects as devices for demonstration and evaluation, while the states regard them as actual policy changes. States are reluctant to allow their "experiments" to be discontinued, arguing that a successful initiative deserves to remain in operation after the researchers are finished with their evaluation. States also argue that their beneficiaries suffer an unnecessary loss of continuity of care when these projects are halted.

The participants suggested that detailed plans for phasing projects out be required in future waiver requests. This requirement would emphasize that the project is an experiment, not a policy change, and would also provide a means for transition at the end of the demonstration.

A Note on the Book

This book was edited by Janet A. Schilling
and Gertrude Kaplan of the
Publications Staff of the American Enterprise Institute.
The cover was designed by Pat Taylor.
The text was set in Palatino,
a typeface designed by Hermann Zapf.
Harper Graphics, Inc., of Waldorf, Maryland, set the type, and
Edwards Brothers, Inc., of Lillington, North Carolina,
printed and bound the book,
using permanent, acid-free paper made by the Glatfelter Company.

Selected AEI Publications

The Health Policy Agenda: Some Critical Questions, Marion Ein Lewin, ed. (1985, 126 pp., cloth $16.95, paper $8.95)

Evaluating State Medicaid Reforms, Pamela L. Haynes (1985, 36 pp., $4.95)

Incentives vs. Controls in Health Policy: Broadening the Debate, Jack A. Meyer, ed. (1985, 156 pp., cloth $15.95, paper $7.95)

Securing a Safer Blood Supply: Two Views, Ross D. Eckert and Edward L. Wallace (1985, 153 pp., cloth $16.95, paper $8.95)

Medicaid Reform: Four Studies of Case Management, Deborah A. Freund, with Polly M. Ehrenhaft and Marie Hackbarth (1984, 83 pp., paper $5.95)

Controlling Medicaid Costs: Federalism, Competition, and Choice, Thomas W. Grannemann and Mark V. Pauly (1983, 112 pp., cloth $13.95, paper $4.95)

• *Mail orders for publications to:* AMERICAN ENTERPRISE INSTITUTE, 1150 Seventeenth Street, N.W., Washington, D.C. 20036 • *For postage and handling, add 10 percent of total; minimum charge $2, maximum $10 (no charge on prepaid orders)* • *For information on orders, or to expedite service, call toll free* 800-424-2873 *(in Washington, D.C., 202-862-5869)* • *Prices subject to change without notice.* • *Payable in U.S. currency through U.S. banks only*

AEI Associates Program

The American Enterprise Institute invites your participation in the competition of ideas through its AEI Associates Program. This program has two objectives: (1) to extend public familiarity with contemporary issues; and (2) to increase research on these issues and disseminate the results to policy makers, the academic community, journalists, and others who help shape public policies. The areas studied by AEI include Economic Policy, Education Policy, Energy Policy, Fiscal Policy, Government Regulation, Health Policy, International Programs, Legal Policy, National Defense Studies, Political and Social Processes, and Religion, Philosophy, and Public Policy. For the $49 annual fee, Associates receive

- a subscription to *Memorandum,* the newsletter on all AEI activities
- the AEI publications catalog and all supplements
- a 30 percent discount on all AEI books
- a 40 percent discount for certain seminars on key issues
- subscriptions to any two of the following publications: *Public Opinion,* a bimonthly magazine exploring trends and implications of public opinion on social and public policy questions; *Regulation,* a bimonthly journal examining all aspects of government regulation of society; and *AEI Economist,* a monthly newsletter analyzing current economic issues and evaluating future trends (or for all three publications, send an additional $12).

Call 202/862-7170 or write: AMERICAN ENTERPRISE INSTITUTE
1150 Seventeenth Street, N.W., Suite 301, Washington, D.C. 20036